TEXAS BIGFOOT

History, Legends, and Modern Encounters in the Lone Star State

LYLE BLACKBURN

legend
SCAPE

An Original Publication of LegendScape Publishing

Texas Bigfoot:
History, Legends, and Modern Encounters in the Lone Star State

Copyright © 2022 by Lyle Blackburn

ISBN: 978-1-7349206-4-2

Cover art by Claudio Bergamin

Illustrations by Claudio Bergamin unless otherwise credited

Photos courtesy of individual photographers as credited

Edited by Beth Wojiski (bethwojiski.com)

Proofreading by Jerry Hestand

Print design by Lyle Blackburn

For more information about the author, visit:

lyleblackburn.com

facebook.com/lyleblackburn.official

twitter.com/BlackburnLyle

instagram.com/lyleblackburn

youtube.com/user/MonstroBizarro

*"I'll be somewhere down in Texas
if you're lookin' for me."*

- George Strait

CONTENTS

Foreword.. 1

Introduction.. 3

1. **Legendary Tales** 7

   Wild Woman of the Navidad 12

   Austin Area Ape Things.................................... 15

   Hairy Man of Round Rock 16

   Crockett's Monster 18

   Wild Things of the Early 1900s........................ 22

2. **Trinity Terrors**... 25

   Lake Worth Monster.. 27

   Apes in the Wake 38

   The Mysterious Leg... 41

   Chambers Creek Monster / Athens Banshee....... 43

   Booger County 49

   Incident in Grapeland 51

3. **Red River Rogues**... 55

   Callisburg Troll 57

   Sherman Gorilla.. 60

   Manimals.. 66

   Sulphur River Squatch 71

   Beasts Beyond the Lake..................................... 78

4. **Cross Timbers Creatures**..................85

   Brazos Ape-Man..................86

   Hugo's Monster..................93

   They Always Travel the Creeks 94

   San Antonio Anthropoids 98

   Ape-X 105

5. **Wilder West** 111

   Caddo Critter 112

   Hawley Him 116

   Panhandlers 122

   Bugs and the Bigfoot Murders..................126

   Horizon City Monster 129

6. **The Bigfoot Capital** 137

   Marion County Monster..................139

   Caddo Creature 147

   Sasquatch Cinema..................154

   Tracks in the Midst 156

   Lakes, Pines, and More Signs 159

7. **Sabine Things**..................165

   Panola Phenomenon 167

   The Hog Hunter 173

   Something Is Out There..................178

   Port Neches Photo 183

   Worth the Pursuit 186

8. Big Thicket Beasts..191

    Sam Houston Hairy Ones...............................195

    Caught on Film?..204

    Angelina Ape Files...208

    Marauding Monkeymen 215

    Ol' Mossyback 219

Conclusion...229

Appendix 1:

Names for Bigfoot-Like Creatures in Texas.............233

Appendix 2:

Maps and Data..234

Acknowledgments 239

Sources...241

Index...253

About the Author...259

More Books by the Author 261

FOREWORD

Here I am, writing the Foreword for a book that I should have written myself. It's kind of ironic, but no one, myself included, could have written this book as well as Lyle Blackburn. I first met Lyle when he attended my 2009 Texas Bigfoot Conference in Tyler, Texas. He soon became one of my very best friends. I still remember him attending the event, he looked the part of a rock star, but came across very humble and unassuming. I immediately liked him. Shortly thereafter, I was invited to attend one of his band's shows. His band, Ghoultown, is described as a cross between Johnny Cash and Rob Zombie. It was every bit that, and then some. The humble and unassuming guy from the Bigfoot Conference was not so much on stage! I remember thinking "This dude is a frigging rock star!" And, come to find out, he can also write!

Since then, we've spent a lot of time together, from deliriously road-tripping to the Mothman Festival to commiserating over lunch at our favorite restaurants. But no matter what and where, it's always been good times! We've talked a LOT of Bigfoot, that is no doubt. Lyle has spoken at nearly all of my events since we met and became fast friends. And for that, I am eternally grateful.

All these years later, Lyle has finally collected the subject of many of our Texas Bigfoot discussions, and well beyond, into a book that is surely long overdue and, in my opinion, important. Of the U.S. states with the most reported sightings, Texas ranks anywhere from fifth to seventh for most sightings in Bigfoot report databases. To the layperson, that is probably hard to believe. Most people think of the Pacific Northwest when they think of Bigfoot or Sasquatch. Yet Texas easily ranks in the top ten for number of reported sightings. I've personally talked to more than three hundred people over the years that claim they've seen a Bigfoot. Of those, I feel a good percentage were describing an encounter that actually took place. Even if I threw out all of the witness testimony I've heard, I had my own personal experience that took place on May 30, 1994, on a lonely, dark road in the neighboring state of Louisiana. Bigfoot is certainly out there.

Lyle and I have always had fun together, researching Bigfoot and other cryptids, collaborating on television shows, and even dreaming up our own ridiculous cryptids for laughs and giggles. So it's an honor to write this Foreword because I know this book will be an excellent read, just like all of Lyle's other books!

Love you like a brother, buddy!

Craig Woolheater

July 1, 2022

INTRODUCTION

When most people think of Texas, Bigfoot is probably not the first thing that comes to mind, or even the second. Tales of the Alamo, cowboys, oil tycoons, and legendary football games are more likely to crop up in conversation than what most would consider a mystery best suited for the forests of the Pacific Northwest. Yet Texas is a vast place full of strange anomalies that are often as big as its ten-gallon reputation, and that includes sightings of ape-like creatures fitting the description of Bigfoot. From haunted ghost towns to spook lights to prehistoric birds and even Bigfoot, the Lone Star State boasts a healthy history of mysteries sure to rival that of any other place across North America. And that makes sense because it is indeed a BIG place.

As a lifetime resident of Texas, even I wasn't initially aware of the massive amount of strange tales that have become a part of the state's quirkier side of history. I was born in Fort Worth, a town that typifies what many nonresidents think of when they ponder the Lone Star landscape. It's located in the northeastern part of the state and was originally established as a trading post at the end of the Chisholm Trail, where cowboys stopped to rest, trade goods, and get rowdy before they set out on another cattle drive. In many ways it's come to represent the Texan stereotype with its cowboy-hat-wearing citizens, saloons and steakhouses, and location on a rolling plateau where wooded areas are broken by long stretches of prairie grass, dry creeks, and nothingness. This seems perfect for tales of haunted hotels and ghost towns, but hardly an environment where one would expect to see a Bigfoot.

They say "everything's bigger in Texas," and that seems to be true. The state encompasses many varied ecoregions and has plenty of big surprises when it comes to its legends. At its western border, near the historic town of El Paso and the Rio Grande River, the landscape is an arid desert where tumbleweeds roll aimlessly in the hot wind. Here we can find reports of mysterious lights on the horizon and massive flying creatures that would seem more at home in the age of dinosaurs. Across the central portion of the state, the landscape begins to mirror a Hollywood western where a drive through the countryside will likely include sightings of longhorn cows amid various forms of cowboy hats and ranch hands. You might also see strange, hairless canids running the roads at dusk and purported goatmen lingering near bridges. As the land sprawls to the east, pine trees began to crowd their way into the scenery until it becomes one huge expanse of towering trees and greenery. Here, tales of phantom felines and Bigfoot-like creatures are all too common as they circulate all the way down to the sloshy shores of the Gulf Coast. Second only to Alaska in square miles of forestry, these wild areas of Texas offer plenty of trees, creeks, thickets, and even swamps where mysterious creatures may indeed roam and flourish.

I found this to be true as my family attended reunions in my grandmother's hometown of Carthage, which lies at the far eastern edge of the state in an area known as the "Piney Woods." Unlike the rather open expanse of my hometown in Fort Worth, this region is completely engulfed by pine forests that create a vast canopy of backwoods grandeur and deep shadows. The environment here seems completely at odds with the stereotypical cowboy landscapes that one might picture if they haven't traversed the full geo-wonderful expanse of the massive state. As we drove to and from those gatherings, I would spend hours staring into the endless trees wondering what mysterious things might be lurking among them. Little did I know that some of the most dramatic sightings of ape-like creatures in North America had long been circulating among those evergreens. It was something the locals may have known, but until the proliferation of the internet, few outsiders probably realized.

In the years to come I would fully delve into this subject, as I researched and documented various Southern Bigfoot cases from old legends to modern sightings. I was initially sparked by the classic stories from the Pacific Northwest, as many cryptid researchers are, but it's the southern tales upon which I have focused most of my attention, partially because of my Texas roots, but also because I found the reports of these alleged creatures to be just as valid and compelling as those from the customary Bigfoot country.

The subject of Bigfoot, however, is not something that can be neatly divided into boundaries—whether North, South, state by state, or even by countries. This is a worldwide mystery that has captivated people from all cultures and creeds as the stories evolved from Native tales and early legends to well-documented incidents investigated by serious-minded individuals. If you are reading this book you may well know that Bigfoot creatures have been reported by a wide range of credible individuals whose testimony lends credence to the possibility that something like this could exist in modern times. And if it does exist, then it could just as easily exist in the vast thickets and swampy bottomlands of Texas as it can anywhere else. The state is home to bears, cougars, and other rarely seen fauna, so why not Bigfoot? Once you travel this land, you will find that nothing here seems too improbable or ultimately impossible. Even the Alamo's most celebrated hero himself, Davy Crockett, may have encountered a Bigfoot during his own travels. It's a story that most people don't know, but one that is firmly planted deep in the heart of Texas Bigfoot lore. If everything is bigger in Texas, this may well be the state's biggest—and most unexpected—mystery of all.

1.
LEGENDARY TALES

Dusk was creeping into the thicket as Dan Ryan approached a small creek in the Sulphur River Bottoms of East Texas. He had been hunting in the area for the last few weekends, but on this particular evening he was looking for arrowheads along the waterways that fed off the banks of the Sulphur. He found two exceptional arrowheads by chance, so on this occasion he'd left his hunting stand to search for more.

Ryan was in an area near Bassett just south of the Red River, a massive waterway that carves a boundary between his home state of Texas and Oklahoma to the north. The woods along the Sulphur River were thick and teaming with wildlife. It was the early 1960s and the region was sparsely populated, making it a perfect place for hunting, boating, or searching for Native American artifacts.

The day had been warm and humid, but as evening approached a wave of cooler air descended to create a light fog that started to settle into the bottoms. It created something of an eerie atmosphere, yet it was oddly pleasant as the last chirps of the afternoon birds gave way to the serene sounds of evening.

Ryan approached the creek bed and began scanning the muddy bank for signs of artifacts. As he looked down, an odd feeling urged him to look up. When he did, he was startled to see a tall figure standing on the bank of the creek approximately forty yards away. It just stood there as if it were watching the hunter in a cautious, wary fashion.

Ryan felt the hair on the back of his neck rise with a cold chill. At first glance, he thought the shape was that of another hunter, but as he looked closer, he could see otherwise. The figure was standing upright on two legs—somewhere between six and seven feet tall—yet it had a thick body that looked to be completely covered in dark hair. Its arms hung lower than a human's would from thick shoulders that blended into its neck like a football lineman. Longer hair fell from its head, framing the dark mass of its face. The forehead and jaw were pronounced, but it was hard to make out the full details of its face. From what Ryan could tell, it looked like a cross between a human and an ape.

The shocked hunter wasn't sure what do to. He had never seen anything like it before and had no way of knowing whether it was dangerous. The creature appeared to be studying Ryan as it moved its head forward. He got the impression the creature was old, as if it belonged to some ancient world that had long been forgotten. The dusky light, combined with the foggy haze, gave the entire scene an otherworldly look.

"It was probably only a few seconds total, but it seemed like minutes," Ryan told me of the encounter. "I was literally frozen, wondering what kind of thing I was looking at."

Suddenly, the thing turned and walked into the trees beyond the creek bank, striding on two legs the entire time. In seconds it was out of sight. Ryan could not discern any noise from its footsteps, nor could he hear any birds. He realized the woods had gone completely silent.

Ryan immediately turned and scrambled back the way he had come, away from the creek and through the darkening woods. He was worried the creature might follow his noisy footfalls, but he had no choice. He just wanted to be out of the woods as fast as he could.

The hunter eventually made back to his car and quickly drove out of the area. He watched the road closely in the beam of his headlights but did not see the thing again. And that was okay. The experience had been completely unnerving.

Ryan was unfamiliar with the concept of Bigfoot at the time and had never heard any of the early stories coming out of the Pacific Northwest. Even if he had, it would not have been something he connected to his home state of Texas—not in the least. He'd been hunting since he was a teenager and was familiar with the outdoors and what it might hold. This, however, was something altogether unexpected and shocking. He would have liked to believe it was a bear, but he knew it wasn't. And if it wasn't a bear or a human, then what else could it be? He would ask himself that question for years until he finally heard tales of Bigfoot and the "Boggy Creek Monster" out of southern Arkansas. As he shared the story with me, I could sense he was still pondering the very question of "What was it?"

Sightings of similar ape-like creatures have long been reported in the Lone Star State, though most people probably don't realize it. Texas is certainly not known for Bigfoot, even though it ranks among the top states where Bigfoot is likely to be seen, judging from the various online Bigfoot report databases. This thinking undoubtedly stems from the impression that Texas is primarily filled with ranches and cowboy landscapes where such a creature would have little chance of existing undiscovered. Texas, however, is a very diverse place where a wide assortment of creatures, large and small, can and do proliferate. And if we place stock in the incredible amount of reports documented in the state, then this fauna may include Bigfoot or some variation thereof.

This supposition might not be as surprising as it seems. As far as potential habitat, Texas is only second to Alaska in total acreage of forest land. The eastern portion of the state, where much of the forest land is located, boasts upward of twelve million acres alone.[1] The rest of the state, while made up of varying ecoregions of coastal marshes, prairies, grasslands, desert valleys, and arid plateaus, also offers plenty of rugged, remote, and natural environments. Bigfoot encounters have been reported in more than sixty-six counties in Texas, and with each passing year there are more reports, especially in the eastern portion where the ecological conditions are most suited for such a thing.

The phenomenon of the Southern Bigfoot, including Texas, is not exclusive to modern times. Native American legends dating back hundreds of years often describe similar large, hairy creatures that were said to lurk in the piney woods and swamp-lands of the South. The Caddo Indian tribe, who were the first to populate the convergent areas of eastern Texas, Louisiana, and Arkansas, spoke of a race of large beings who inhabited the woods. According to Kathy Strain, archaeologist and author of *Giants, Cannibals, and Monsters: Bigfoot in Native Culture*, they referred to them as the *ha'yacatsi,* which translates to "lost giants."[2] While we can't be sure these are equivalent to the modern-day Bigfoot or even flesh and blood creatures, it does establish the possibility that the early inhabitants experienced similar encounters.

The Choctaw tribe of the American Southeast, whose modern-day lands now include an area in Southern Oklahoma (just miles from where Dan Ryan encountered a creature in the 1960s), told of a creature called Shampe. The creature was said to be a malevolent monster, sometimes described as a giant and sometimes as a large, hairy man.[3] Shampe was often accused of eating men or abducting women. The creature's most prominent characteristic was its smell. The odor was so overpowering a person could not bear to be around it, making it difficult to confront the creature. Some stories also say that Shampe makes a whistling sound as it stalks through the woods.[4] When the Choctaw were relocated to Oklahoma from their original native lands in the regions of modern-day Mississippi, Alabama, Louisiana, and Florida, they believed Shampe followed them.

Though again, it's hard to know whether the stories of Shampe were based on an actual living creature or just a part of Choctaw mythology, the characteristics of the tall, hairy form, horrible odor, and whistling ability are very much related to Bigfoot, especially in the South where these creatures are often referred to as "Skunk Apes" because of their pungent odor. Bigfoots are also thought to use whistling as a method of communication, making Shampe a good candidate for the equivalent of our modern-day phenomenon.

From the earliest Texas stories and legends, there seems to be a record of strange, upright, and hairy creatures stalking the woods and waterways. The thing Dan Ryan saw in the 1960s is not new or surprising, though its presence in a state known for so many things other than Bigfoot may have been overshadowed in the past. But as the modern era of written history progressed, the tale of Bigfoot in the Lone Star State would eventually rise to cast its own tall shadow over the land.

Wild Woman of the Navidad

One of the earliest cases of a possible Bigfoot-like creature in modern Texas comes from Lavaca County located in the southeastern portion of the state. Known as the "Wild Woman of the Navidad," the details were recorded by early newspapers and later disseminated by author J. Frank Dobie in his book, *Tales of Old-Time Texas*.

As the story goes, settlers living on the banks of the Navidad River near Texana began to notice odd, barefoot tracks around their homesteads in the year 1837. These were usually two sets of human-like footprints with one set being larger than the other, as if to suggest a male and female. As time went on, the larger tracks ceased to appear, leaving only the smaller tracks, which began to increase in frequency. This led to the locals dubbing the mysterious track-maker the "Wild Woman."

Over the span of several years, the tracks of the Wild Woman were often found around homes where items and trinkets were stolen, though no one actually saw "her." The settlers organized occasional searches to find this mysterious woman, whom they thought of as either a feral person or perhaps some kind of strange animal that had human-like feet. On one occasion, a party driving cows through the river bottom came upon a "den" that was believed to be the home of the Wild Woman. There they found a "variety of little trinkets, such as pins, needles, knives, and brushes" along with some guns, books, and "several articles whose uses were entirely unknown."[5] These items had been collected in some kind of basket found in the den. The article, originally printed in the *Victoria Advocate* (Texas), does not explain why the party did not wait there or return there in an attempt to see or apprehend the alleged Wild Woman. A reward of "forty cows and calves" had supposedly been offered to anyone who could capture the mysterious creature, so it would seem like a lucrative effort to wait. Regardless, more searches for the Wild Woman ensued, but no one was able to catch her or even get a glimpse because she was apparently able to move with great stealth through the woods and bottomlands.

Sometime between 1845 to 1850, a small hunting party resolved to catch the Wild Woman once and for all. A telegraph sent from Houston, Texas, to the *Daily Sanduskian* in Ohio, conveyed the story:

> *Mr. Glasscock pursued it [the Wild Woman] for several days with dogs, and at one time approached so near it as to cast a lasso upon its shoulders. It, however, with great adroitness eluded the snare, and fled to a dense thicket where it could not be traced. Mr. Glasscock states that he was near a small prairy [sic] enclosed by the border forests of the river, when the creature emerged from the woods and ran across the prairy [sic] in full view. It was about five feet high, resembling a human being, but covered with hair of reddish brown color. In its hand it held a stick about six feet long, which it flourished from side to side, as if to regulate its motions and aid it when running at full speed. Its head and neck are covered with very long hair, which streamed backward in the wind. It ran with the speed of a deer, and was soon out of sight. The dogs pursued it, and came so close upon it at a small creek,*

that it was compelled to drop its stick, which was taken by its pursuers.

Several other persons have repeatedly seen the creature, and they all concur in representing it as a human being, but so covered with shaggy hair as to resemble an ourang outang [sic].[6]

The descriptions of the Wild Woman seem very much like a small "Bigfoot," but another telegraph from Houston dated March 17, 1851, claims the Wild Woman had finally been caught by some deer hunters. They described her as a woman of African descent who had fled to the wilds more than fifteen years earlier. They said she could not speak English but could apparently speak to other Africans.[7]

Navidad River bridge in Lavaca County
(Photo by Lyle Blackburn)

The resolution seems to contradict the previous description of the Wild Woman being completely covered in hair and resembling an orangutan, so it's hard to sift out the truth of the matter in this old story. Regardless, these reports mark the first in recorded history where people of Texas claimed to have seen an upright creature covered in hair roaming the thick, piney woods of the state—and it would certainly not be the last.

Austin Area Ape Things

Twenty years after the sensational story of the Wild Woman, another strange report sprang from the brush country of Central Texas. According to the September 1, 1871, edition of *Argus* news, an "immense orang outang [*sic*]" had been seen near Gatesville, north of Austin. It was described as being "seven feet high and covered from head to foot with a thick coating of hair."[8] The creature had eyes that shone like "fire" and a "double row of murderous looking teeth." When it was last seen, the alleged primate was said to be carrying a large stick in its hand and a calf under its arm. A hunting party was organized to capture or kill the monster, but no details about its success, or lack thereof, are included.

In 1875, the *Austin Democratic Statesman* ran an article about a "Wild Boy" who was caught by men on horseback in nearby San Marcos. The "strange being," who was described as being fearful and aggressive, apparently had a body "covered with hair about four inches long."[9]

Both reports are strange and hard to accept at face value—given the strange details such as fiery eyes and murderous-looking teeth—yet still raise an eyebrow when considering the case for early Bigfoot reports.

Terrain in the vicinity of Austin
(Photo by Lyle Blackburn)

Hairy Man of Round Rock

A strange tale that often arises when discussing the subject of Texas Bigfoot is that of the Hairy Man of Round Rock.
Round Rock is located north of Austin in the central portion of
the state, not far from the aforementioned towns of Gatesville
and San Marcos. According to the tale, a young boy was traveling
with a group of settlers sometime in the 1800s when he became
separated. A storm had blown in during the night causing a
nearby creek to rise. As the group was trying to escape the water,
he became lost in the woods.

The rest of the settlers eventually moved on, leaving the
hapless boy to survive on his own. Over the years he became more
feral and supposedly grew hair over his entire body as he existed

alone in the woods surrounding Brushy Creek. He took on the appearance of a frightening, hair-covered beast, and when anyone would pass by, he would terrorize them by emerging from the woods. This habit ultimately led to his tragic end, however, when he jumped out to frighten a passing stagecoach. The startled horses veered toward him and trampled him to death.

The road where this supposedly happened, south of Brushy Creek, was officially named "Hairy Man Road" by the developing town of Round Rock. Over the years, people who traveled the shadowy thoroughfare at night were said to have encountered a large, hairy man lurking in the trees alongside it. In modern times, the road has become a destination for teenage thrill-seekers who dare to challenge their wits against the legendary Hairy Man.

The city of Round Rock has grown considerably over the years, so the location of the road is not as remote as it once was. But the legend is still strong. The city hosts an annual Hairy Man Festival in October that features music, food, crafts, and other activities including a "hairiest man" competition. In 2017, the Round Rock State Park launched a playful campaign to entice visitors by claiming that park rangers had spotted a Bigfoot there and had even found tracks.[10] They invited kids to come out and help the rangers track down the elusive creature, or as locals referred to it, the Hairy Man.

The urban legend aspect and playful Bigfoot campaign have muddied the truth as to whether Bigfoot is actually lurking in the area. The location seems far too populated and cut off from any sufficient woods that would be necessary to host a large, unknown creature at this point, yet the question still lingers. Was this legend based on an actual hair-covered *man*, or could it be attributed to an unknown, ape-like beast who once inhabited the sparsely populated area of Brushy Creek years ago? We will never know.

Hairy Man Road in Round Rock
(Photo by Craig Woolheater)

Crockett's Monster

When I was a kid, my hero was Davy Crockett. In Texas, he is a prominent figure who fought in the famous battle of the Alamo, where a small band of volunteer fighters faced off with the massive Mexican Army in an attempt to gain Texas's independence from Mexico. The Texan fighters, whose ranks numbered a mere two hundred, held off thousands of highly trained Mexican soldiers for thirteen heroic days in the spring of 1886 until they were at last defeated. David Crocket, along with other notable fighters such as Jim Bowie and William Barrett Travis, all perished in the battle but have since become the famous heroes of Texas independence.

Crocket, who was originally from Tennessee, was one of the

most recognizable of the Alamo fighters with his buckskin clothes and signature coonskin hat. His frontier image and participation in the Alamo came to symbolize the rugged, woodsman-turned-freedom-fighter attitude that embodied the early American spirit. Just about every souvenir shop around Texas sold coonskin hats, and as a kid I proudly wore one as I often reenacted Alamo battles with my neighborhood friends. Little did I know that once described seeing an ape-like "apparition" or monster that sounds very much like a Bigfoot!

In a letter addressed to his brother-in-law, Abner Burgin, Crockett wrote:

> *William and I were pushing through some thicket, clearing the way, when I sat down to mop my brow. I sat for a spell, watching as William made his good and fine progress. I removed my boots and sat with my rations, thinking the afternoon a fine time to lunch. As the birds whistled and chirped and I ate my small and meager ration, I tapped my axe upon the opposite end of the felled tree I rested upon.*
>
> *Whether it was the axe's disturbance or possibly the heat of the high sun which caused an apparition to slowly form in front of my eyes, I know not. As a Christian man, I swear to you, Abe, that what spirit came upon me was the shape and shade of a large ape man, the likes we might expect among the more bellicose and hostile Indian tribes of the Territories. The shade formed into the most deformed and ugly countenance. Covered in wild hair, with small and needling eyes, large broken rows of teeth, and the height of three foundlings,[i] I spit upon the ground the bread I was eating.*

---

i   A "foundling" is a small child said to have been abandoned by his parents.

The Monster then addressed a warning to me. Abner, it told me to return from Texas, to flee this Fort and to abandon this lost cause. When I began to question this, the Creature spread upon the wind like the morning steam swirls off a frog pond. I swear to you, Abner, that whatever meat or sausage disagreed with me that afternoon, I forswore all beef and hog for a day or so afterward.[11]

Crockett seems clear in his narrative that it was an apparition or spirit, yet even so, why and where would he get the idea to describe something like a large ape-man? It's a truly bizarre footnote in the life of what is arguably one of the most famous men associated with Texas.

David Crockett
(DeGolyer Library at Southern Methodist University)

Wild Things of the Early 1900s

Reports of wild men and other hairy horribles continued to pop up in various parts of Texas well into the early 1900s. On February 9, 1933, *The News* (Port Arthur, Texas) reported that a long-haired, shaggy "wild man" was spotted near a cave in Newport (northwest of Fort Worth). A group of explorers, headed by P. B. Cox, had been making daily trips to the densely wooded hills where this person or thing had been seen. On one occasion they saw the wild man, whom they referred to as a "Tarzan," dash from the cave and "nimbly scale a cliff above the primitive dwelling and speed through dense underbrush with the alacrity of a wild animal."[12]

Another Texas Tarzan was reportedly seen along the Brazos River near Richmond in April 1933. Sheriff Rusk Roane told newspapers the "wild man," who inhabited the thickets outside Houston, was something like a "Tarzan of the Apes."[13] A search was to be mounted in order to flush out the strange forest dweller, but no information about its result was published.

Around the same time, a rather frightening wild man was seen outside a schoolhouse in Ellis County south of Dallas. The details were relayed to me by Josh Turner, curator of a small natural history museum in Cleburne, Texas. He said that in the early 1930s his grandmother, Pauline Beaty, was a child living the small town of Cedar Hill. The area was heavily wooded in those days, and there had been several sightings of what her family referred to as the "wild man." One afternoon while Pauline and her classmates were having recess outside their one-room schoolhouse, two of the boys ran back inside screaming in terror. They told the teacher they had seen a big, hairy man lurking at the edge of the woods. The teacher, realizing it was no joke, quickly ushered all the students into the schoolhouse and locked the door. After some frantic discussions, two of the older boys volunteered to go for help. There was no phone at the schoolhouse, so this required them to bravely run on foot to the town. While the boys were gone, the teacher and students could hear thrashing, screaming, and ranting from the woods. By the time help arrived, however, whatever had been there was gone.

In 1938 another spooky incident was said to have taken place a mere nine miles east near the town of Red Oak. According to the report, four men were coon hunting one night in the heavy woods surrounding Red Oak Creek. As they sat in camp waiting for their dogs to sniff out a raccoon, they noticed the dogs weren't barking as they usually did on the hunts and were instead sitting close to the fire acting scared.

"About that time they noticed a huge white haired figure standing about 30 or so yards from the fire," one of the witnesses' sons wrote. "It was just standing there watching them."[14]

The frightened hunters quickly grabbed their guns and dogs and fled from the bottoms. The next day they told others of the encounter, but no one believed their story. "My father was a very honest man . . . and I know his story to be true," the son affirmed.

The report is admittedly secondhand, but it does support the notion that Bigfoot-like sightings have been occurring in Texas for many years. This particular report is also unique in that it specifies a white-haired entity. This is extremely interesting in light of the numerous accounts that would eventually spill out of nearby Lake Worth some thirty years later. The story of the Texas Bigfoot, it seems, was just getting started.

2.

TRINITY TERRORS

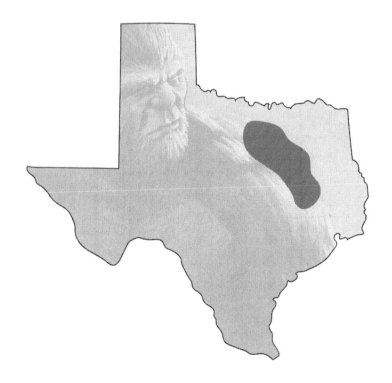

As the 1900s ticked past the midcentury mark, more and more tales of strange, ape-like creatures were creeping out of the Texas countryside. In some cases, the reports emanated from areas of Central and North Texas—with sprawling metroplexes and lack of mass forestry—that would now seem ill-suited for Bigfoot. At the time, however, this area was less populated, and much of it still wide-open country with cities spaced leisurely in between. The region is also intersected by a number of river corridors, a common ingredient in many Bigfoot encounters. The creatures have often been reported near rivers, creeks, lakes, and swamps, not just in Texas but everywhere.

The proximity of Bigfoot sightings to waterways makes a lot of sense, especially in the South where the temperatures can be hotter. Such creatures would obviously require copious amounts of water to simply survive. The waters of a river not only provide hydration but ensure the proliferation of vegetation and animal life critical to the diet of any large animal.

Waterways also create a "path of least resistance" through wooded areas and public lands, potentially allowing such creatures to move from one feeding area to another as they struggle to survive in the often-harsh terrains of the South. The areas of rivers, creeks, bogs, and bayous also tend to remain less disturbed by human development, thus providing an environment where something could live and move in relative seclusion.

It is not surprising that many of the Bigfoot-type reports in Texas have occurred along the Trinity River corridor. This significant waterway cuts a long, snaky path as it runs from North Texas all the way south to the Gulf of Mexico. Along the way it occasionally spills into lakes and reservoirs or flows a lonely path through wide-open countryside where the winds whisper with mystery. Over the years the Trinity River corridor has produced some of the most dramatic accounts in all of Texas Bigfoot history, including that of the infamous Lake Worth Monster.

Lake Worth Monster

On July 10, 1969, the widely circulated *Fort Worth Star-Telegram* newspaper ran an unusually bizarre story with the headline "Fishy Man-Goat Terrifies Couples Parked at Lake Worth." The article, written by journalist Jim Marrs,[ii] detailed an incident involving six people who claimed they were assaulted by a scary, hairy creature while sitting in their cars along the banks of Lake Worth in the early morning hours.[15]

John Reichart told police he and his wife had been parked near the lake with two other couples when something leaped from a nearby tree and landed on their car. The thing, which he described as "half-man, half-goat with fur and scales," tried to grab his wife, but he managed to start the car and drive off before it got ahold of her. Reichart drove to a nearby café where he called police. When patrolman James McGee and his partner showed up, Reichart was visibly shaken, and so was his wife. Something had definitely frightened them.

After listening to the bizarre story, the officers followed Reichart outside the café, where they saw an eighteen-inch scratch down the side of Reichart's car. Reichart said the creature had made the scratch while trying to grab his wife. Officers then escorted the couple back to the location where the attack had taken place near what's known as Greer Island. They searched the area but found no evidence of the attacker. Whatever it was, it was long gone.

"We did make a serious investigation because those people were really scared," McGee told Marrs. Officer McGee said his department had been receiving calls of a similar nature since June, but until that morning they had simply been brushed off as a joke. After investigating the claim by Reichart and the other couples, the police concluded it must have been the work of a "prankster."

---

ii Jim Marrs would go on to write several *New York Times* bestsellers on the subject of conspiracies.

The area where the attack occurred was essentially a Lover's Lane hangout where local teens and couples came for the purpose of privacy or to "party." It was located in the heavy woods surrounding Lake Worth, about ten miles northwest of Fort Worth. The lake, then and now, is a reservoir on the west fork of the Trinity River that flows across North Texas. It was created in 1914 not only as a site for storing water, but also for recreation. Back in those days, there were various dirt roads that led down to the lake. The main hangout was at the end of Shoreline Road where it dead-ends at Greer Island, a small patch of land cut off from foot access by the water. The area was altogether remote and dark, perfect for couples to find seclusion, and perhaps, perfect to conceal an unknown creature. It was here the attack took place.

The fact that police wrote the incident off as some kind of prank did not stop the public from becoming completely enthralled after reading the monstrous details in the *Star-Telegram*. The article, along with radio and television reports, created such a stir that people began to assemble at Greer Island the next day, hoping to confront the "goatman" themselves. By the evening of July 10 (literally the same day as the Reicharts' early morning attack), there were as many as forty people—including members of the Tarrant County Sheriff's Department—gathered near a landmark across from the island known as "The Pit," when some kind of thing appeared on a high ridge above. It began to run back and forth in the thick brush, avoiding the trail that ran down to the ridge. Witnesses said it let out a "pitiful cry" before it eventually threw a heavy tire (which included the rim) an estimated four hundred feet above the heads of the shocked onlookers.

The crowd was so alarmed, most of them immediately fled. One young man reportedly backed his car into a tree as he tried to get away. Others waited with guns drawn, but the thing disappeared into the vast trees atop the ridge. Luckily no one was hurt during the chaos, which was a very real possibility given the firearms and panicked crowd.

The following day, July 11, the *Star-Telegram* ran a follow-up article that recounted the details of the incident. Those who had seen the thing on the ridge described it as a large creature with gray or white hair on its body much like a goat. Some of the witnesses believed they also saw horns. A man by the name of Jack Harris told reporters "the creature walked like a man but didn't look like one. He looked like he was seven feet tall and must have weighed about 300 pounds."[16]

These bizarre descriptions create a sort of cryptozoological conundrum since some of the traits would place it into the so-called "Goatman" category, while others would lump it into more of a "Bigfoot" category—if, of course, it wasn't a person in a costume.

The ridge overlooking the "pit" where the alleged
Lake Worth Monster was sighted

(Photo by Lyle Blackburn)

It was dusk outside, but in this case numerous people got a good look at the thing as it ran along the ridge and threw the tire. They did not believe it was simply a person dressed in a costume. I recently interviewed Clydell McPeak, who was actually on the top of the ridge that night. McPeak told me he didn't see the thing throw the tire, but a short time later he did see it walking off into the woods. He said it was big, covered in hair, and didn't seem to be a human.[iii]

As a result of the news articles, various public officials began to weigh in with theories to explain away the monster. In a *Star-Telegram* article dated July 14, a representative of the Fort Worth Museum of Science and History stated that he believed the "monster" to be a bobcat.[17] A naturalist at the Greer Island Refuge and Nature Center backed him up, saying that a pet bobcat had been turned loose in the area at one time. A bobcat might account for the "pitiful cries," but by no means can a cat of any size throw a tire four hundred feet over the heads of thirty-plus witnesses.

Another theory was offered by a local kennel owner who said he was "tracking a 40-pound runaway macaque monkey near the lake," but this, too, ignores the fact that witnesses had seen a much larger, bipedal-type creature.[18]

In the weeks that followed, there were more incidents that involved the alleged monster. On one occasion it was seen running across an open grass field. In another, five people claimed they saw it breaking the limbs of a huge oak tree. Others said they heard the thing scream with an eerie sound at night. A young man by the name of Ronnie Armstrong, who was also a witness to the incident on the ridge, claimed the creature had been wounded by a gunshot. He said he followed a trail of blood leading down to the water's edge, where it presumably swam over to Greer Island to escape. Armstrong also saw some tracks that were discovered by

---

iii McPeak was compelled to contact me because he saw me on the "Lake Worth Monster" episode of the *Monsters & Mysteries in America* television show.

three individuals while walking around the lake. The tracks measured sixteen inches long with a toe spread of eight inches. They appeared to have been made by a very heavy, unknown animal. Based on the sightings and tracks, Armstrong felt it might be "a big white ape of some kind."[19]

Most of these later incidents were either ignored or unknown to the press because they were never covered. But luckily, a local Fort Worth resident and would-be writer by the name of Sallie Ann Clarke saw the value of following up on the story. Shortly after the incidents made headlines, she headed to Lake Worth and began interviewing witnesses and documenting the events. She then wasted no time in typing up the story and self-publishing a book called *The Lake Worth Monster* in the early fall of 1969. The book includes interviews with witnesses that would have otherwise been lost.

One of the people who told Sallie about an encounter was Vic Franklin of Fort Worth. He told Clarke it was at least seven feet tall and looked like a "real hairy human." Another eyewitness, Jim Stephens, told Clarke the thing jumped on the hood of his car one night as he and two other men were driving around the lake. They had heard about the creature while fishing that day and decided to look for themselves. Stephens said the creature remained on the hood until he swerved and ran into a tree. At that point, the thing "jumped off and ran into the woods." He described the creature as "real big and human-like with burnt scars all over its face, arms and chest."[20]

Clarke's book is ultimately a semifictional treatment of the subject that includes both facts and interviews with witnesses along with fanciful passages in which she imagines what it would be like to see the creature herself. This approach tends to muddy the waters in terms of accurate, cryptozoological facts, but Clarke's intention at the time was to document the events while at the same time writing an entertaining book. Ironically, she would later have the opportunity to see the creature for herself as she continued her research beyond the book's publication.

In an interview with Sean Whitley, producer of the documentary film *Southern Fried Bigfoot*, Clarke stated that she ended up seeing the monster a total of five times. On the first occasion, Clarke said she was at the lake when she found a "big track." Later she was sitting in the back of a friend's camper when she saw the creature through the screen door.

"I put a metal plate with some shrimp in it on the back of the camper, and that thing come up and stood there, and carried off the plate," she recalled. "I watched it. Boy, I mean, that thing scared the devil out of me. It was just a big, tall white thing."[21]

Clarke lamented that she didn't have a camera with her at the time, but fortunately someone did capture an image of the alleged beast. On November 19, 1969, Fort Worth resident Allen Plaster was driving on Shoreline Drive with a couple from the nearby town of Weatherford at around 1:30 a.m., when one of them saw a large, white figure stand up near the road. Plaster, who was driving, grabbed his Polaroid camera and managed to snap a picture. The resulting photo shows a blurry white figure standing in the grass near a tree.

Allen Plaster showed this photo to Sallie Clarke, who agreed it could be photo of the actual beast. Plaster took her to the place where the photo had been taken. It appeared the subject had been standing in a ditch next to a tree. Using the tree as a height reference, they estimated that the subject in the photo was around seven feet tall. In 2005, Clarke told my colleague Daniel Perez that Allen was an honest person who did not drink. She felt sure he didn't fabricate the photo as some kind of hoax. Plaster and the other witnesses had truly seen something that he was able to photograph.

Plaster later downplayed the photo in a 2006 interview with the *Star-Telegram*, saying he believed that whatever it was *wanted* to be seen, suggesting it might have been someone in a costume.[22] But that was his opinion in hindsight. Plaster has since passed away, and he never did divulge the real names of the other passengers who were in the car with him that night, so it's been impossible to get their perspective on the matter. As it stands, it's one of the better cryptid-related photos that's ever been taken.[iv]

Just weeks before Plaster took the photo, a man claimed to have been attacked while he slept in the back of his truck near Greer Island. On November 7, 1969, Charles Buchanan set out for a day of fishing on the lake. Later that night he decided to sleep there in the back of his pickup truck. He told reporters that around 2:00 am he was awakened when he felt his truck moving as if someone was trying to shake it or tip it over. Then suddenly, a hair-covered face appeared over the side of the truck bed followed by two long, hairy arms. They were reaching for Buchanan, who was inside his sleeping bag. Thinking fast, Buchanan reached for some barbeque chicken he had left over from dinner and shoved it toward the beast. The thing promptly let go of the sleeping bag and shoved the chicken in its mouth before running off toward the lake. It then plunged into the water and swam in the direction of Greer Island. Buchanan described it as about seven and a half feet tall with long arms and short, stubby fingers. He said it was probably seven hundred pounds and looked like a cross between a human and a gorilla or ape; in other words, very much like a Bigfoot.[23]

As 1969 came to a close, monster fever around Lake Worth began to dwindle as the sightings diminished. Some folks, such as Sallie Clarke, continued their research, but for the most part the

---

iv As far as I know, the original photo was given to Sallie Ann Clarke and is now in the possession of her family. Luckily, some good copies were made of it. The *Star-Telegram* has one in their files, and a friend of mine bought one of Clarke's books online, and it came with a mysterious copy of the photo. Those are better quality than what mostly turns up on the internet. You can do a Google search on the Lake Worth Monster to view the photo.

newspapers moved on and so, perhaps, did the monster.

In the years that followed many speculated as to what really happened at Greer Island that summer. A number of people claimed credit for a grand hoax, as often occurs in these cases. According to a 2009 article from the *Victoria Advocate*, back in 1969 police questioned several students from a high school in Fort Worth who were found with a "faceless gorilla outfit and a mask."[24] Their identities were not given. In 2005, the *Star-Telegram* received a letter from an unnamed person who claimed he and two friends "decided to go out to Lake Worth and scare people on the roads where there were always stories of monsters." The writer said they used "tinfoil" to make a homemade mask.

The problem with the tinfoil mask and gorilla costume (which would have probably been black or brown at the time) is they don't match the white creature the majority of eyewitnesses reported. However, other claims accounted for this by saying the creature frenzy was inspired by a goatskin or carcass displayed on the hood of a car or thrown down from trees onto the vehicles of couples who were parked below. But that just doesn't make sense either, because if it landed on the car, it would just lay there unmoving. It wouldn't have tried to grab Mrs. Reichart and pull her from the car or try to pull Mr. Buchanan from his pickup. And it wouldn't leave tracks.

To evaluate yet another rumor, a reporter from *Fort Worth Magazine* tracked down a man by the name of "Vinzens" who claimed credit for the tire-throwing incident.[25] According to the article, Vinzens affirmed that on July 11, he and two other guys had gone to Greer Island to party, and they ended up on the bluff overlooking The Pit and the throng of monster seekers below. In an innocent attempt to "fire up the festivities" and impress some girls, he and his buddies rolled a tire down the bluff. He said it looked more like a "toss" because there was a bump toward the bottom of the bluff that launched the tire into the air. Vinzens said that "when the incident made the papers the following day, he and his friend decided to lay low" to avoid any repercussions from police or the armed monster hunters who were stalking the area day and night.

Interesting, but Vinzens is not the only person to take credit for the tire toss. A woman named Jan Galloway told a blogger at the *Domain of Horror* website that her brothers were responsible for all the "goatman" incidents. "They tied ropes and grapevines off in the day time [*sic*] and at night my younger brother Jack Shelby [11 years old] wore my rabbit coat and they would fly across the hoods of the cars and barely touch the hoods," Galloway claimed.[26] "One night my brother Billy Shelby [15 years old] decided to come across the ground on all fours like a monkey . . . he jumped on top of a car and scratched the windshield and made a Tarzan sound and jumped off."

Billy's prank supposedly sent the first couple to call police. Later, she said, Billy put on cut-off shorts and a white t-shirt, then smeared a "black eye pencil" on his face, arms, and legs. After ascending the ridge at Greer Island, he and several boys used a "giant slingshot" to launch the tire across the pit while Billy beat his chest and made more Tarzan sounds.

With so many ridiculous claims, it's hard to sift out the truth in the matter, be it a man or monster. The only certainty is that strange things were going on at Lake Worth and there were witnesses who believed they saw something that was not a human in a costume. To add to the mystery, sightings in the area didn't start in 1969. For years people had talked of a creature that haunted the lake. Some called it the "Mud Man" or "Mud Monster," while others simply referred to it as a ghost. A resident who had lived there for forty years told Sallie Clarke he saw something like the Lake Worth Monster at least twenty years earlier.

When the Lake Worth Monster made headlines in 1969, it became known as a "Goatman." Over the years, however, it's become more associated with Bigfoot lore. A so-called Goatman, in terms of cryptids, is a different kind of creature than a Bigfoot. Goatmen are often described as looking more like a goat with horns, fuzzy hair, and possibly hooves, except they are able to stand on two legs like a human. Most Goatman legends revolve around bridges, almost like a troll figure from traditional folklore. What is described in the Lake Worth Monster case is much more of a large, ape-like creature with white hair. The white hair could be one reason it was associated with Goatman lore, along with the first headline that literally referred to it as a "Fishy Man-Goat."

Could the Lake Worth Monster have been a rogue Bigfoot with white hair? There have been reports of Bigfoot creatures in that general area over the years. In 1963, the *Denton Record-Chronicle* reported someone near the town of Denton claimed to have seen a "hairy, eight-foot thing" which the locals referred to as a "monster."[27] The details are sketchy, but Denton is a mere thirty miles north of Lake Worth.

There was also the previously mentioned incident from 1938 where some coon hunters claimed to see a huge, white-haired figure near Red Oak. Red Oak is only forty miles from Lake Worth.

I got a secondhand report from Tinia Smith who told me her father, Robert Kirkeby, saw what he described as an ape with white hair while hunting in Decatur back in the 1950s. Decatur is a scant thirty-five miles from Lake Worth. This description definitely fits the profile of the Lake Worth Monster and, like the others, occurred in the years prior to the publicity of 1969.

Sightings of a white-haired creature continued for a short period after 1969 and then ceased, leading many to question whether the thing was ever there or if it had perhaps moved on down the river. There have been no recent sightings either, but that's certainly understandable. Lake Worth is a very different place now than it was back in the sixties. The wilderness surrounding the lake has given way to considerable development. The only thing that remains is a three-hundred-acre nature preserve that surrounds Greer Island. That's still wooded, but it's within a stone's throw of fast-food restaurants, shopping centers, and busier marina docks where people enjoy water sports. The creature may be long gone, but the Lake Worth Monster has become a permanent part of local Fort Worth history, and it seems it is just one piece of a larger, hairier puzzle.

The author at Greer Island holding a copy of Clarke's book
(Photo by Craig Woolheater)

Apes in the Wake

In the summer of '69, as the frenzy was brewing in Lake Worth, two teens encountered a similar entity in Ellis County only forty miles away. According to one of the witnesses, he and a friend decided to have a picnic on his friend's farm near Sardis. The area was heavily wooded with some open pastures and creeks running through the property, making it a nice place for an isolated, outdoor respite.

The friends drove to the location in the late evening, bringing their food, a rifle, and his friend's German shepherd. They found a spot in an open area near a pond surrounded by tall reeds, where they sat down to enjoy their meal. As they were eating, however, the dog began to act strange. It started pacing back and forth and growling. The witness could see the hair on the dog's neck stand up as it looked toward the pond and started barking. According to the witness:

I looked around and when I looked toward the pond, there was an ape-like creature that appeared to be observing us. At the time, I didn't want to believe what I was seeing. It was an ape-like creature but not an ape. The way I think of it now is that it looked like what you would think a very ancient, primitive man might look like, but still retaining some ape-like qualities. It was just getting dark but was not completely dark, so I can't describe certain details such as facial features. Maybe I can't remember some of the details because I was so frightened. It had its right arm outward and away from its body, holding the reeds to one side and just appeared to be observing us. It was very powerfully built, especially in the shoulder and chest area. It was covered with hair and looked like it had no neck. The left arm was hanging down at its side and it extended to a length to its knees.[28]

The teens were completely overtaken with fright. The witness's friend yelled, urging him to get to the car. They grabbed the essential items and dashed to the vehicle with the dog close behind. There was a gate to the property, so they had to stop and open it before they could drive out. When the witness's friend got out to open and close the gate, they were both apprehensive, thinking the ape-like creature might suddenly appear. They drove as quickly as they could from the area, never looking back.

Whatever the teens saw, perhaps, had been lurking along the Trinity River corridor for years. Just twenty miles northeast of Lake Worth sits Grapevine Lake, where another interesting incident occurred a decade earlier. Floyd Fry, whom I met during a book signing I did in Fort Worth, told me he and his family were picnicking at Grapevine Lake in the late 1950s when he discovered something unusual.

As with Lake Worth, Grapevine is now developed, but at the time it was surrounded by woods. Even the picnic sites, which were new at the time, were simply clearings cut from the thick trees. Fry was about eight years old, and having no similar-aged playmates present, he was left to wander around by himself.

"I wasn't paying attention and went farther than I thought away from my parents," he told me. "That's where I found some giant-sized footprints in the sand."

The footprints came from a tree line, crossed an open area of freshly cleared land, and disappeared into the trees on the other side. "Even as a child, what struck me was the size of the prints," Fry recalled. "They were huge, barefoot prints, and I knew they were too large for a normal man. My thought was they must have been made by a giant."

Apprehensive yet curious, Fry followed the footsteps into the woods along what appeared to be a game trail. "I lost the footprints there but continued following the trail for a short way among the trees," he said. "But I became too frightened and turned back."

Young Floyd ran back to where his parents were still enjoying their picnic. He told them what he had found and urged them to look, but they brushed it off thinking he was joking or exaggerating. At the time Fry didn't connect the event to Bigfoot, but in retrospect he wonders if such a creature could have been responsible for the seemingly impossible imprints.

Another witness in the area had a shocking imprint left on her young mind. While researching the Lake Worth case, I came across a woman by the name of Cynthia Dunston, who told me of a possible Bigfoot encounter she had in 1982 near Eagle Mountain Lake just a few miles north of Lake Worth. She was young at the time and was visiting her grandparents, whose house was located on the lake. She spent many afternoons exploring the woods surrounding the home, and on this occasion she had followed an old cow path from their barn to nearby Ash Creek.

"I got about halfway down the path when I saw something," she told me. "There was a dark shape in front of the fence at the end of the path."

Cynthia, a rather experienced outdoorswoman for her age, felt there was no reason to be alarmed, so she kept walking. As she got closer, however, the shape moved and she could see it more clearly. "Then I froze," she recalled. "I knew exactly what it was."

Standing before her was a hairy, man-like creature. "I remember that its hair was longish and a dark auburn color," she told me. "It looked as tall as an average man but not freakishly tall."

To her understanding, Bigfoot did not *eat* people, so she was not completely panicked as she observed the thing. "This was more like extreme apprehension and caution of a large animal when you don't know what it is going to do," she recalled. "This appeared to be a natural animal."

Despite her faith in the creature's benign eating habits,

Cynthia turned and started back toward the barn. She didn't want to run, thinking it might give chase, but hurried at a good pace nonetheless.

"When I was almost to the barn, I looked back," she continued. "It had followed me but stopped past the halfway point where I had been standing before. As soon as I had the house in sight, I made a wild dash for the gate to the backyard. Safely inside the gate, I looked back toward the barn. There was nothing there."

The Mysterious Leg

In 2013, I investigated strange—if not disturbing—report from a horse breeder who once owned a ranch in Grand Prairie. The property was located along the west fork of the Trinity River, south of the Dallas/Fort Worth area. In a phone interview, Floyd Ramsey told me he was working on his ranch sometime around 1974 when he noticed his dogs were chewing on something. Upon closer inspection, he discovered it was a huge, hairy leg severed at the knee joint. The ragged appendage was covered in dark, coarse fur similar to that of a bear, but it had a human-like appearance and a human-like foot with five toes. If the leg were standing upright, Ramsey said the knee would have come up to his mid-thigh. He estimated the foot would be a "size twenty-two" in human terms. Ramsey assumed his dogs had dragged it up from the Trinity River Bottoms.

Puzzled and concerned, he made a call to the Dallas County Police. In due time, two officers showed up and inspected the leg. They were equally puzzled. As per standard procedure, they confiscated the evidence for further examination, but promised Ramsey they would let him know about their findings.

Ramsey eventually received a follow-up call from the department, but it was only to report that examiners couldn't determine what kind of "animal" the leg had belonged to. They could only confirm it was not a bear or human. Ramsey never heard from the police again.

Nearly forty years later, Ramsey was watching an episode of *Finding Bigfoot* when he thought of the bizarre incident. In 1974 he didn't consider the possibility of Bigfoot, but in retrospect it seemed like a possible explanation. Like Lake Worth and Grapevine, Grand Prairie has been consumed by the greater Dallas-Fort Worth metroplex, but at the time it was still rough and wooded where such a creature could have roamed, especially with its proximity to the Trinity River.

The Trinity River
(Photo by Lyle Blackburn)

In order to check out the story, I wrote a letter to the Dallas Police Records Archive requesting a copy of the police report. I didn't have an exact date or case number, so it was a long shot, but worth a try. The Dallas Open Records Department eventually returned a letter stating they could not find the report. They questioned why the Dallas police responded instead of the Grand Prairie police, but Mr. Ramsey was positive it was Dallas officers who came to his ranch that day.

The hairy leg story sounds fantastic and unquestionably falls into a category of reports in which promising evidence seems to mysteriously disappear once it's in the hands of authorities. But even so, I found Ramsey to be very well spoken and credible. I had no doubt he had once been in possession of the leg. Too bad for the sake of Texas Bigfoot, it has disappeared into the governmental void.

Chambers Creek Monster / Athens Banshee

Moving further south along the Trinity River corridor we eventually cross a long, lonely body of water called Chambers Creek. The creek, which spans sixty-seven miles through Ellis and Navarro Counties, is said to be the home of a Bigfoot creature known as the Chambers Creek Monster. In the first public report, a man claimed that his father, Kenneth W., and a friend were fishing along the creek between the towns of Avalon and Ennis in 1964 when "a large, hulking, hairy creature, approximately eight to ten feet tall appeared before them and roared."[29] The men panicked and quickly made their way out of the creek bottoms.

Aside from his father mentioning an old sighting from the 1930s, it was thought to be an isolated incident until researcher Larry Parks tracked down additional witnesses who claimed to have seen something similar near Ennis. According to Parks, the first instance occurred around 1964 when several people were camping near Chambers Creek's low-water crossing at Ensign Road. While cooking fish, they heard something large approaching through the brush. As it got closer, they heard a distinct growling and smelled a putrid odor. When the thing finally emerged, the campers saw that it was a big, hair-covered creature like a Bigfoot.

The second incident occurred a few years later, around 1969. In this case a group of young men were walking in the woods near Chambers Creek when they heard a strange animal sound. They looked around and saw "an 8–9 foot tall, hair-covered creature drop down on all fours and charge towards them with a strange gait." They said it had really long hair and definitely wasn't a bear.[30]

In 1977, a Corsicana newspaper reported two sightings near the Richland-Chambers Reservoir on the east end of the creek. On August 22, three women were driving on Highway 274 when they saw a "hairy man-like creature." They were so startled they reported the sighting to the local sheriff. The second encounter occurred on September 2. In this case, a man was driving on Highway 31 when he saw a seven-foot creature run across the road.[31]

Twenty years later, strange things were still stalking the area. In April 1998, a family saw a large, upright entity cross the road in Henderson County just a few miles east of the Richland-Chambers Reservoir. It was a warm, muggy night, and a woman and her son were driving through a heavily wooded area. Suddenly, the woman caught sight of a large figure standing in the ditch on one side of the road. She had just rounded a sharp curve and presumably surprised the strange lurker. She slowed down and watched as it quickly crossed in front of the headlights, moving on two legs and taking large strides. The "animal" looked to be approximately seven to eight feet in height with a massive head and a body completely covered in hair. The thing proceeded in the direction of a lake where it stopped at the wood line. The son looked up in time to see it peering at them from behind a tree before it turned and walked into the darkness.[32]

The witnesses were interviewed by researcher Mike Hall,

who felt they were credible and truthful in their story. The son remarked that: "It was taller than the van we were riding in, and was moving in an upright manner the entire time like a man but was not a man."

The witnesses had been en route to check on their new house, which was currently under construction a short distance away. After they encountered the thing, the mother quickly turned the car around and left the area. She did not want to risk another encounter, especially in the darkness of their new, rural property.

The woman noted that she had been compelled to report the sighting to the Texas Bigfoot Research Center website because she had learned of another report where a family living less than two miles from the location of their encounter had experienced a series of truly bizarre and frightening incidents a decade earlier. According to this family, they were living on a twenty-seven-acre property near Athens in the years of 1989 and 1990 when the incidents occurred. One of the witnesses, "Amanda," who was a teen at the time, said the family consisted of her mother, brother, and sister-in-law. They lived in a rental house on the property that included a pond surrounded by woods and open pastures.

Shortly after they moved in, the family began to hear strange noises in the woods surrounding the house. The most prominent of the noises sounded like an eerie, howling scream. The mother dismissed it as the calls of a wild cat and, at first, they thought it was funny because the sound would often scare visitors. The family jokingly referred to it as the "banshee." But things became much less humorous when they began to catch glimpses of some kind of large, white-looking thing in the woods.

The first person to see the thing was a boy who lived nearby. He had come over one night in the summer of 1989 to visit Amanda. As they were talking out back, the guest suddenly had a shocked look on his face. When Amanda asked him what was the matter, he said he had just seen a "large white figure moving from tree to tree hiding behind them."[33]

The second person to see something was Amanda's boyfriend. His truck had broken down while visiting her, so he decided to walk home through the fields since he did not live very far away. He said a "large white figure walked beside him" all the way to a fence at the edge of the property. The boy was so afraid, he just kept looking forward and did not try to look directly at the figure for fear it would attack him.

Amanda finally encountered the thing herself when she was walking down a road one night with a friend. "[This] thing came from behind a tree, ripped a huge tree limb off and threw it," she recalled. "We were so frightened. We turned and ran."[34]

Amanda outran her friend, who said he could feel it breathing down his neck as they fled toward his house for safety. They jumped over the gate in front of his property where several more of their friends were standing. They all noticed "something white" had been pursuing them but then suddenly disappeared in the dark woods.

On other occasions the thing had been seen by additional visitors to their property and by a neighbor as he rode his ATV through the backwoods.

Prominent Texas Bigfoot researcher (and cofounder of the Texas Bigfoot Research Center), Craig Woolheater, interviewed Amanda, who he said was initially hesitant to share the story for fear of ridicule. Eventually she opened up and told Woolheater everything that she could remember about the harrowing experiences while living on the secluded rental property. She said the subject in question had been seen occasionally over the two-year period up until they moved as a result of the scary activity. Amanda described the banshee thing—or creature—as being around eight feet tall with white hair all over its body. She estimated it probably weighed between two hundred fifty and three hundred pounds. The family initially thought of it as a ghost, but it seemed more like some kind of creature judging from the movements and the presumably connected vocalizations. She said that when they heard the howl, the animals in the vicinity would begin to react wildly out of fear and nervousness.

While the true nature of this entity is hard to pin down, it is interesting that it appeared to be covered in white hair. It seems that many of these incidents along the North and Central areas of the Trinity River support the notion that the famous Lake Worth Monster may have been much more than the fevered imaginations or hoax work of local teens back in the Summer of Love. Whatever was stalking the area was unique but certainly not alone in the greater context of the legendary Lone Star Sasquatch.

Illustration by Joshua Foster

Booger County

Between the Trinity River and the Brazos River, southeast
of Waco, lies the county of Robertson. It would normally be a
rather innocuous stop on the Texas roadmap, except in this case
the region has been nicknamed "Booger County." Before the
term Bigfoot was used in the South, the word *booger* was often
used to identify any such large, hairy, human-like beast that was
said to live in the deep woods and thickets. While this could be
interpreted as many things, from undefined monsters to were-
wolves to forest imps, most have associated it with Bigfoot. The
association could have been based on an actual sightings by the
residents or tales told for generations by their family, friends, and
neighbors. Many rural Texas residents may recall their grandparents' warnings about so-called "boogers" who lurked in the
woods. They'd say "Get home before dark, or the boogers will get
you."

As such, it has been suggested that Robertson County's
mysterious nickname could be the result of Bigfoot sightings in the
area. And there certainly have been some. According to a report in
the Gulf Coast Bigfoot Research Organization database, a witness
claimed that a "large ape man" attacked his home near the town of
Calvert in the early 1970s. He claimed that the creature even tore
off a piece of his roof during the incident. Gulf Coast Bigfoot Research Organization (GCBRO) founder, Bobby Hamilton, noted
that: "Locals have referred to this area as 'Booger County' for a
long time due to the creature that was roaming around there."[35]

In another incident, a farmer was reportedly attacked
while working on his farm outside of Calvert. According to the
report, the man was plowing some crops in the early 1970s when
he noticed something moving along the tree line at the edge of
his field. As the farmer moved closer on his tractor, an "ape man"
emerged from the woods and advanced toward him. When it got
close to the tractor, it tried to crawl onto it. The farmer jumped

off and retreated to safe distance. From there he watched the animal as it moved around on the tractor for a period of time before jumping off and walking back into the woods. He described it as being "7-8 foot tall, brown, covered with hair." He said it "walked like a man, but was more of an ape man in appearance."[36]

During the same time period, yet another incident supposedly occurred in the Brazos River Bottoms west of Calvert. A man was riding a horse along the edge of a tree line when the horse became spooked. It turned and started bolting away despite the rider's attempt to get the animal under control. The rider glanced back, at which time he saw an "ape-like creature" pursuing them. The horse eventually out-distanced the ape-thing and calmed down. The man described the entity just as the farmer had: "Ape like in appearance, walked and ran on two legs, brown in color, 7-8 foot tall."[37]

Outside of these documented reports from the 1970s, other vague tales suggest that something large and hairy has continued to roam the area. In 2007, a woman supposedly saw a "naked 'man' covered all over with dark hair" as she was driving at night on a rural road. The woman was startled by the incident but watched carefully in the rearview mirror as she drove off. The thing remained standing in the road.[38]

There's no question that Robertson has long been known as "Booger County," but is Bigfoot the reason? Some historians have suggested it was the result of notorious highwaymen (thieves), while others propose it's the result of some child pranksters who lived in the area at the turn of the twentieth century. Whatever the case, there have been some rather dramatic tales of ape-like creatures in the area, and that's enough to lead one to wonder.

Incident in Grapeland

The Trinity River corridor is long and winding and full of tales that seep from its muddy banks like an endless stream. Sometimes these come in the form of old legends or hearsay, while sometimes they come directly from a person whose perspective has been significantly altered by a chance encounter. Craig Wortham is one of those individuals.

Wortham told me that in November 2007, he and his wife had traveled to Grapeland (just east of the Trinity River near the Davy Crockett National Forest) for a Thanksgiving celebration with her family. After enjoying the meal that afternoon, Wortham's brother-in-law, Kevin, asked if he wanted to take a drive out to the ranch he managed. Wortham agreed, so they jumped in Kevin's truck along with Kevin's father, Bruce.

It was around 4:00 p.m., and the sun was still playing out the last hours of a clear, sunny day. The ranch was about four miles outside of town along a county road, so it didn't take long to get there. When they arrived, Bruce got out and opened the property gate while Kevin drove the truck through. After the vehicle passed, Bruce closed the gate and got back inside of the truck. Suddenly, all three men noticed a huge creature standing thirty yards away at the edge of a tree line that ran parallel to the road. It was upright on two legs and was covered in dark brown hair. As soon as they saw it, the thing sprinted toward the road and across it, then disappeared into the trees on the other side. It looked to be at least nine feet in height and moved bipedally the entire time, leaning forward slightly as it ran. It appeared to be headed toward a small creek that branched off the Trinity River and ran through the property.

"All of this occurred very fast," Wortham explained to me. "All three of us watched the crossing, and we just sat there, truck running, in total shock."

The thing cleared the road in three huge steps. "He was

dark brown, almost black, with four to five-inch-long hair," Wortham said. "He had no neck, and his arms were huge and long and swinging as he ran. His torso was just massive and thick."

A few moments later, Wortham began to laugh as he realized what they had probably seen. It was a combination of excitement and disbelief. He asked the other two men "What did ya'll just see?" Their reply was just as he expected.

"After a few seconds, Bruce said 'I always knew they were here, but now I know.' Kevin couldn't even talk. A few more minutes passed and Kevin said . . . 'Well, it wasn't a man in a monkey suit, and it wasn't a bear, so that leaves' . . . and I said, 'Come on, say it!' Then we all agreed we *had really* seen a Bigfoot!"

During the encounter, the men noticed a lack of normal woodland sounds; no birds chirping, no breaking twigs—just a strange stillness and silence. It was altogether odd, but there was no doubt in Wortham's mind that he and his relatives had truly encountered a Bigfoot.

"Needless to say, [Kevin and Bruce] said they refused to tell anyone other than family about the incident because everyone would say they are nuts, and they feared for their jobs," Wortham concluded. "I am an ex-peace officer in Texas and have been trained notice details. And as I live and breathe, I will never forget that moment."

It is doubtful anyone could forget such an encounter. Sometimes legends do come to life.

Wooded area near the Trinity River

(Photo by Lyle Blackburn)

3.

RED RIVER
ROGUES

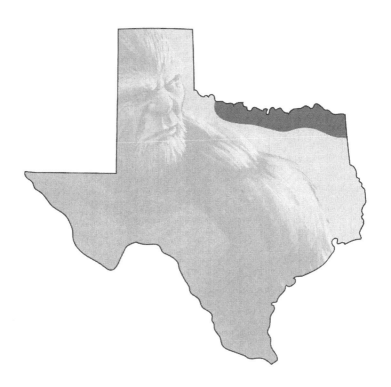

At the northern end of Texas, where the southern low hills of Oklahoma meet the border, lies the striking Red River. This waterway, with its distinctive red, ferric oxide tint, is the second-largest basin in the southern Great Plains, flowing along the border between Oklahoma and Texas and extending across several ecoregions as it moves into southwest Arkansas and on into Louisiana, where it feeds the Atchafalaya River. Upon its path, the river winds through scenic lands of high plains, piney woods, and southern swamps.

The Red River has been a crucial ingredient in the settlement of the area, starting first with the Caddo tribes who inhabited its banks long before the Europeans arrived. The river naturally provided plenty of game and fish, as well as fertile lands where crops could be cultivated. As the Europeans moved in, the river became a significant route for travel by boat.

The Red River has also played a significant role in the history of our mysterious Texas wild ones. As we've already noted, such rivers offer access to water and usually wind through areas of lush forestry where seclusion can be found. Not surprisingly, a great number of Texas Bigfoot sightings have occurred along the Red River and its many tributaries that branch off like a veiny web into the wilds. Wilds that extend into other Bigfoot hot spots in states such as Arkansas and Louisiana.

The fact that sightings along the river have taken place not only in Texas, but in the other states where it flows, seems to offer credibility to the concept of Southern Bigfoot as a whole. In other words, this is not a phenomenon exclusive to one state, but something that extends outward from the common sources of waterways and woodlands.

Perhaps the most significant example is the association between the Red River and the famous case of the Boggy Creek Monster. The Boggy Creek Monster, or "Fouke Monster," is a Bigfoot-like creature said to roam the bottomlands near the small town of Fouke in Southwest Arkansas. Sightings of the creature are not unlike many of those we've already examined, except in this case the creature achieved a much higher level of fame due to a movie called *The Legend of Boggy Creek* released in 1972. Produced and directed by Texarkana filmmaker, Charles B. Pierce, this hybrid docudrama / horror movie effectively dramatized sightings of the creature that occurred in the 1960s and early 1970s in and around a small tributary in Fouke known as Boggy Creek. The movie was an unexpected hit, and it picked up nationwide circulation in 1973, played to countless audiences who were both enthralled and frightened by the story. The movie was so widely circulated in theaters, drive-ins, and eventually on television that it reportedly raked in nearly $25 million dollars in revenue.

Though the film is not set in Texas, it is import to our story since the infamous Boggy Creek is tied to the Red River basin where many Lone Star Sasquatch have also been reported. Boggy Creek originates in Fouke and eventually flows into the Sulphur River which, in turn, joins the Red River in Southern Arkansas. The Sulphur River, along which there have been numerous classic sightings of the Fouke Monster, actually originates in Texas where similar sightings have taken place. These ties tend to strengthen the case for both the Texas Bigfoot and the Fouke Monster, offering a level of credibility. In other words, if these creatures do exist then they would surely be seen throughout the expanse of any given tributary where they are known to roam. And this is exactly what we have in the case of these hairy, scary Red River Rogues we are about to examine.

Callisburg Troll

An interesting cluster of Red River Bigfoot sightings can be found in Cooke County, Texas, near the site of an old bridge. The bridge, which spanned Sandy Creek, was built in 1893 to accommodate wagon passage to and from the town of Callisburg.

The now historic bridge was recently relocated to Callisburg Park due to its age, but not before it could garner an esteemed reputation for being haunted by more than one sort of strange entity. According to an article published by the *Gainesville Daily Register* in 2004, "The 1893 bridge is one of the four oldest in the state. Local officials wanted to keep it because of its history, which includes ghost and Big Foot [*sic*] stories as well as its age." [39]

Some of the ghostly tales involving the bridge seem well rooted in urban legend and teenage pranks, but there have been a number of credible witnesses who attest to the presence of ape-like creatures. My friend and colleague, Jerry Hestand, who has been actively researching the Bigfoot phenomenon since 2001, has personally investigated some of these accounts. According to Hestand, there seems to be a pattern of Bigfoot sightings between Grayson County and Cooke County along the Red River.

One of these encounters allegedly occurred in the winter of 1976. The witness, who was a teenager at the time, said he was standing on the Texas side of the Callisburg bridge watching ice float down the river when he heard what sounded like coon dogs chasing something on the Oklahoma side. As they came into view, he could see two hounds on the trail of some kind of huge, hairy animal. The animal ran on two legs but did not appear to be human.

The young man watched as the creature jumped over a fallen log and plunged into the surrounding brush. The lead dog followed and began yelping a few seconds after it went out of sight. The second dog followed, but immediately turned around and ran back in the direction it had come. The first dog fell silent and never reemerged.

Frightened, the teenager jumped on his motorcycle and sped home. He later mustered enough courage to return to the location but never saw the strange beast again.

Hestand interviewed the witness (now an Army veteran)

in 2004 and found him to be credible. "The witness seemed sincere in his statements," Hestand stated. "There was no doubt in his mind as to what he saw. The witness claims the animal was about one hundred fifty yards or so away, and he saw it for only two or three seconds, but he was sure it was not human."[40]

More recently, around 1993, a young woman was outside her home in the Hagerman Wildlife Refuge (approximately fifteen miles east of Callisburg) when she got the shock of her life. It was late spring, and a storm was rolling in during the early nighttime hours. Her father had just driven off in his Jeep, and she was standing on the front porch. Suddenly, she got an eerie feeling that someone or some*thing* was watching her.

"I turned toward the pasture and there was this tall, lean, lanky, hairy mannish thing coming toward me," she said. "I called quietly to my younger sister because I was terrified."[41]

The thing was looking directly at her with piercing brown eyes as it walked up to a fence surrounding the home and put its hand on a post. By now her sister had come onto the porch and was making a "whimpering noise" as she watched it.

"The fence [was] at least four to five foot tall. He towered over it," she recalled. "He was massive in height. His hair was not like the pictures I have seen [of Bigfoot]. Its hair did not resemble fur; it was coarse, straight, long, dark brown (maybe some reddish coloring to it). He was not like an ape or bear. He was muscular but not bulky."

Her father, who had been out looking for one of their landlord's horses, was now returning down the long drive. The witness looked momentarily at his Jeep, and when she looked back to where the creature had been standing, it had already fled halfway down the pasture. Then it simply vanished in the darkness.

The young woman asked her father if he happened to see anything strange while driving around, but he said he did not. When she told him about what she had seen, he did not believe her and, in fact, punished her for making up such a wild story and scaring her sister. It would be several years before she became aware that creatures such as Bigfoot had been reported in Texas. She had been haunted by the memory of the incident ever since that night. Perhaps now, she at least had an answer.

The historic Callisburg bridge
(Photo by Jerry Hestand)

Sherman Gorilla

In the summer of 1960, residents of the small town of Sherman, just east of Callisburg along the Red River, began bolting their doors and grabbing their firearms as a nervous trepidation gripped the community. A monster was apparently loose, and they weren't taking any chances.

According to the *Sherman Democrat* newspaper, on Monday July 11, J. O. Conrad had just gotten into bed around 10:30 p.m. when something startled his dog.

"I was smoking a cigarette when the dog started barking," Conrad told a reporter. "I looked out the east window and saw him. He looked to be seven feet tall and about three feet wide across the back. He stood upright but hunched over."[42]

At first glimpse, Conrad thought it might be a man. But as he studied it a few moments, he realized it was much too large to be a person. Concerned, Conrad jumped out of bed, grabbed a flashlight and a handgun, and headed toward the front door. Conrad's wife and thirteen-year-old son, James, heard the commotion and quickly rushed to the window, where they observed the thing lurking in the moonlight.

Conrad went onto his front porch and advanced toward the animal, firing at it three times with a .22 pistol. "I know I hit him at least once, but he didn't even flinch," Conrad said. "That's when I went after my shotgun."

In the meantime, Mrs. Conrad phoned the sheriff's office in Sherman and apprised them of the situation. The deputies warned against shooting the animal because they were afraid a bullet wound might cause it to attack.

Mr. Conrad took heed and didn't try hit the animal again.

"I fired the shotgun over his head, but he didn't run, just shuffled off to the east down the side of the highway," Conrad continued. "I jumped in my car and followed. I got a real good look at him in my headlights while I was following him. He looked black as coal. He was real hairy except for his face. I was about 20 feet from him when I shot, and I didn't try to get closer. I was scared."

The hominoid continued, walking upright on two legs all the way to the Blue Creek bottoms east of the community. After it went into the underbrush, Conrad said he gave up the pursuit.

Conrad wasn't the only one to get a visit from the beast. As the community began to buzz about the strange "monster," they compared notes. A Mrs. Curtis Wilson, who lives about one hundred yards east of Conrad, said she and her husband were awakened shortly before Conrad saw the animal. "We heard something rattling around in the shrubbery beside the house and our two dogs were going crazy," Mrs. Wilson recalled. "Then we heard something thump against the house and the dogs hushed."

Mr. Wilson went outside to find the dogs cowering in the corner of the porch. He then heard his cows go into an "uproar." Conrad's shots rang out shortly thereafter, sending Mr. Wilson to fetch his own rifle. By the time he got back outside, however, he could not find the beast.

Resident W. B. Thompson said a man drove into the all-night gas station where he worked, going on about how he'd seen "a large, strange-looking animal along the roadside."

Grayson County Deputy James Spaugh, who answered Mrs. Conrad's call for help, said that as far as he was concerned "Conrad definitely saw something and it wasn't a man." Conrad theorized it might have been a gorilla. He admitted he'd never seen a gorilla before but judging from a picture he and his son found in an encyclopedia, that seemed like the best candidate.

It wouldn't be the first time a nonindigenous animal had been seen in the Sherman area. Police Captain V. J. Brown told the *Sherman Democrat* some years earlier a local resident had been awakened by a "trampling noise" in his front yard. Figuring it was the neighbor's unruly mule, he grabbed a shotgun full of bird shot and headed to the front door. When he opened the door, he found himself "face to face with an elephant." Apparently the creature had wandered away from a circus that was playing in town![43]

While the ape-thing seen by Conrad and the others could very well have been a gorilla, it's interesting that this "primate" walked upright for such a long distance and was purported to be seven feet tall. This certainly sounds more like a Bigfoot than a gorilla, an animal who would typically move on all fours if traveling long distances.

When this news clip came to light in 2017 (thanks to researcher Willie Jacobs), my colleague Jerry Hestand, who lives in Grayson County about ten miles from Blue Creek, headed over there to see what he might be able to dig up all these years later. Miraculously, Hestand hit pay dirt! First, he managed to locate an elderly woman who remembered the incidents well. She told Hestand that at the time (around 1960), her neighbors had been talking about a large, dark animal of some sort that had been haunting the nearby woods for as long as they could remember. The woman said she might have actually seen the animal in the 1950s.

The lady, then a teenager, was walking her dog along the edge of Blue Creek late one afternoon when she noticed a strange structure made out of underbrush and saplings. She approached the unusual structure and saw a huge, black animal laying in it. It appeared to be sleeping or otherwise unmoving. Her dog became anxious and began pulling at its leash, as if to indicate danger. At that point the girl walked quickly from the area. She was not sure what kind of animal it was. She could only recall that it was large, covered in dark hair, and appeared to have built some of kind of nest.

Hestand also located James Conrad, the son of J. O. (James Otha) Conrad, who was thirteen years old the night they saw the "gorilla." Amazingly, James was still living at a residence near Blue Creek! James was sitting in his front yard in a wheelchair when Hestand drove up and introduced himself. James said he remembered the incident well. At the time his family owned a Conoco gas station on the highway and were living behind it. He said he was actually the first to spot the gorilla at which time he alerted his father.

"I happened to be looking out of my window . . . and right beside my window was a gorilla," he explained. "It scared the heck out of me because it couldn't have been more than ten feet away."[44]

James told Hestand that it was "gigantic" and well over six feet tall, maybe seven. It was covered in black hair and was *standing and walking on two legs at all times.* He estimated its weight to be between four hundred and six hundred pounds. After his father shot at it, the animal headed across the highway, once again, on two legs. James said his father then called several neighbors to alert them. Naturally, no one believed him.

James then told Hestand something that seems rather bizarre. "It was an escaped gorilla from a circus or zoo that was in Sherman," he said. "The Grayson County deputies cornered it in Choctaw Creek bottoms and shot it twice with a .38 caliber pistol. Then the animal was corralled into a large cage and was carried back to the zoo/circus."

James said there had been two newspaper articles about the so-called gorilla, one that detailed his family's encounter and a later one that covered the so-called capture. However, at least so far, no follow-up article about a capture has been found in the *Sherman Democrat* archives.

According to Hestand, the details simply do not make sense:

> As I drove away, I was naturally puzzled. I had lived in Grayson County all of my life and I knew there was no zoo in Sherman. I had seen all the circuses that had passed through as a child and I only remember one that had a "gorilla." An elaborate poster showing a monstrous, giant ape tearing at his cage was exhibited outside of the venue. Upon entering the exhibit I saw an undersized chimpanzee that didn't look healthy. (So goes the sideshow exhibit.)
>
> So what did the family see? Was it indeed an escaped gorilla; a huge one that walked on two legs the entire time it was in view, even after being shot at? How could a circus

even handle a large mountain gorilla in a cage? The like-lihood seems slim to me. Is there really another newspaper article? If so, it must be a spectacular one describing the capture of a wild, injured gorilla on the loose! If there was a capture, where did the animal go? Where did the cage come from? Lots of questions.[45]

THAT'S WHERE THE GORILLA STOOD—J. O. Conrad, left, his son James and Mrs. Conrad, look at the spot near their home at Blue Creek where they said a gorilla stood Monday night. Conrad shot at the animal and followed to the underbrush along Blue Creek. (Staff Photo).

*J. O. Conrad and family provide details
of the "gorilla" sighting to reporters*

(Sherman Democrat – July 20, 1960)

And indeed there are many questions. Was this an actual gorilla or was it something else, perhaps something that was unknown to these folks at the time? The concept of Sasquatch would have surely been unknown to these residents of rural Texas back in 1960. So if they did see something that looked like a large ape walking upright, then it could only have been rationalized as a gorilla. It is a mystery that lingers on in the cool waters of Blue Creek.

Manimals

Newspapers of the 1960s continued to document cases of unusual things in the area. *The Paris News* (Paris, Texas) reported that in 1965, a strange animal was seen near the town of Direct in Lamar County, a short distance from the Red River.[46] According to the article, a woman claimed to have seen what locals often referred to as the "Manimal." She was out one evening near her house when she spotted it with her flashlight. Frightened, she hurried back to the house where she and her cousin watched it jump a fence on all fours then stand up on two legs. "It [was] about [six feet, two inches] as it stood up," she told the newspaper.[v]

The woman later found tracks at the scene, which were examined by a game warden. Although they were described as being large, they were also said to have claw marks, leaving some doubt as whether the Manimal falls into the Bigfoot classification. Either way, the article goes on to say that sightings by "oldsters" in the area date back at least fifty years.

In 1976, just a few miles from Direct between Pat Mayse Lake and the Red River, three men were camping one night when they heard something circling the campsite. It sounded like a large

---

v The fact that the woman could make such a precise height estimate makes this report a bit dubious, but that is what was printed in the paper.

animal. After listening to this for a while, one of the men decided to walk up to an observation tower on the nearby dam. As he approached the dam, he saw a large, hairy creature near the guard rail beside the road. Figuring it was the same thing that had been making noises around the campsite, he quickly returned to tell the others. His friends could see something following him as he returned to the campsite, but they could not tell just what it was.[47]

A similar sighting was reported by another individual (who did not know the previous witness) that same year. The witness in this case said that in July 1976, he was sitting on a bridge overlooking Pine Creek (a small tributary of the Red River) with his brother and friend when a large, man-like animal covered in dark brown hair matted with moss rose up out of the water. The witness was sitting on one side of the bridge, while the other two men were sitting on the other side, so only he saw the thing at that moment. When the creature stood up, its back was to the witness but it was very close, within twenty-five yards. The man got up very quietly and went to retrieve a high-powered rifle from their nearby truck. Before he could get back to the spot on the bridge, however, the other two men came running. One of them had also seen the creature and possibly got a look at its face. The man, who was normally tough and unshakable, was nearly in tears, shaking hysterically. The trio quickly left the area.[48]

In 1979, another Manimal sighting took place in the bottomlands surrounding Direct. According to a report filed with the Texas Bigfoot Research Center, two women were driving in the bottoms at night during the first week of deer season. The moon was full and bright, so they could see quite well as they progressed down a one-lane, gravel road. Suddenly, their attention was drawn to a figure moving into the road about one hundred feet ahead. It was on two legs and looked be seven or eight feet tall with a body covered in long, smooth gray hair. The thing continued to walk across the road in a deliberate manner, as if it were in no hurry. It swung its long, hairy arms as it went, much like an ape. Before the women could digest what was happening, the thing stepped over a barbed-wire fence and disappeared into the darkness.

The strange encounter was so frightening, the women didn't dare get out of the car to investigate. The driver told investigator Craig Woolheater that she drove another mile down the road and then attempted to turn around in a wheat field. In the process, the car got stuck. It took the women at least thirty minutes to free the car, all the while worried that the creature would emerge from the darkness and attack them. When they finally drove back out, it was not there.[49]

Aaron Womack could have never imagined he would see something like Bigfoot in Lamar County, Texas, but in 2007 that's just what he saw. Womack said he was at his home about twenty miles from the town of Direct when he noticed something walking across a field adjacent to his house.

"It was tall, about seven foot, and it had brownish-red hair all over," he stated. "[It] walked upright and kind of looked like a tall gorilla, and it swung its arms when it walked."[50]

The thing moved across the field and eventually disappeared from sight into the heavy woods surrounding it. Womack had recently heard about another sighting near Direct and felt this creature might have been the same one. The Manimal first mentioned in the news report of 1965 was apparently alive and well more than forty years later.

Moving east along the Red River, we find more tales in the adjacent Red River County. According to David Holley of the Texoma Bigfoot Research and Investigations Group, old-timers in that area tell of a strange creature or "wild man" that had been seen near Cuthand Creek during the 1960s and 70s. Known as the "Cuthand Critter," it was allegedly seen by farmers and ranchers on several occasions. Holley also heard stories in the 1980s about a "large, hair covered creature who resembles a huge gorilla" seen walking across some pastures not far from Cuthand Creek.[51]

A woman whose family is from the Red River County town of Hooks told me her late father was adamant about encountering a Bigfoot on the river in about 1965 (around the same time the "Manimal" was first reported in the town of Direct). Angie Smith said her father, Larry Jaggears, was hanging out on the bank one night with several friends when he had to relieve himself. He walked into some nearby brush and was proceeding to do his thing when he noticed a pair of red eyes looking at him. He also smelled a horrible odor. He called out, thinking it was one of his friends trying to scare him, but there was no response. He quickly zipped up and walked toward the eyes. As he did, the eyes moved from behind the brush. At that point he could see a large, bipedal creature that stood at least eight feet tall. Jaggears turned and ran for the safety of his friends. They investigated but found no further trace of the creature.

In April 1982 two boys claim to have seen a Bigfoot-like creature near Bagwell in Red River County. According to one of the boys, he and his cousin were sent by their aunt to fetch their uncle, who was working in a pasture. It was starting to get dark, so the boys hurriedly jumped a fence and started toward their uncle in the distance. When they got within fifty feet, however, they came to the stark realization that the figure standing there was *not* their uncle. It was, instead, a hairy, man-like creature between six and seven feet tall.

"It turned around to look at us, grunted and ran toward the woods," the boys said. "We screamed as it turned."[52]

The animal jumped a fence and disappeared into the dusky twilight just as their uncle came out of a nearby barn to investigate the commotion. He did not believe their story . . . until one evening eight months later. That evening, they were headed off to see a movie in town. It had been raining and sleeting most of the day, so the gravel road of their rural home was sloshy. As they drove carefully away from the house, the boy's aunt suddenly screamed.

"We looked up in time to see it," the boy explained. "It was crossing the road right in front of us. It jumped across a ditch on the side of the road and disappeared into the woods. In the headlights, the color of the animal was that of a brown bear. He was covered with hair. There were missing patches of hair on the arms and legs. Again he seemed to be about six and a half feet tall, kind of sloped up the back."[53]

The witness also said a man who lived near their uncle's house, deeper in the woods, reported seeing a similar creature. "One night he woke up when he heard something rummaging around in the trash barrels out back," the witness said. "He got his shotgun and went outside to shoot what he thought was going to be a raccoon. To his surprise, he was face to face with the creature. [It] grunted and ran away with great speed."

Just eight miles east of Bagwell, near Clarksville, two women were surprised by a strange creature in May 1999. Jeanine and Luci (last names withheld per request) were returning from a trip to Oklahoma around dusk when a rust-colored, bipedal animal emerged from the woods and ran across the highway in front of them. It was "moving in a hunched over position like a man walking into a high wind," as it cleared the road in approximately four huge steps.[54] They could not be sure it was a Bigfoot but, given the numerous reports in the area over the years, it was a possibility.

The Red River in North Texas
(Photo by Lyle Blackburn)

Sulphur River Squatch

Moving eastward, we find the origin of the Sulphur River, a murky tributary that eventually joins the ruddy waters of Red River as the basin begins to turn southward. The Sulphur River, both at its headwaters in Texas and along its tendrils in Arkansas, has a significant history of Bigfoot sightings that ties to the legendary case of the Fouke Monster of *The Legend of Boggy Creek* fame.

I've walked the bottoms and even done extended canoe trips down the Sulphur River and can attest to the wild nature along many of its sections. It's chock full of gators and rife with plenty of hairy creatures such as huge hogs and beavers. It's not a stretch to consider that a few undocumented cryptids might also be lurking on its muddy banks and high ravines.

One of the basin's most publicized Bigfoot incidents occurred in 1969 when two men encountered a creature near a levee
that runs parallel to the South Sulphur River about ten miles from
Commerce, Texas. According to an article in the July 1979 issue
of *FATE* magazine, Kenneth Wilson was in the area around 11:00
p.m. hanging out with three friends. [55] As he sat in his car, his
friends (one man and two women), were out walking along the
levee. Wilson heard something moving in the bushes around him,
then a short time later he heard his friends start screaming. They
rushed back to the car in a panic, saying they had seen something
down by the levee.

Frightened, Wilson drove the group to a nearby gas station
where their friend Jerry Matlock worked. They asked to borrow
his gun. Not wanting to part with the gun, Matlock accompanied
them back to the area to investigate. When they arrived, they were
greeted with a shocking sight as a huge, man-like creature covered
in brown hair jumped over the levee and ran toward the car. "This
thing was bigger than any man I've ever seen in my life," Matlock
explained. "You could have stretched a [3 foot] yardstick across its
shoulders and its shoulders would've been wider than that."

Wilson also got a glimpse of the creature, saying that: "It
was big and hairy, whatever it was." At that point he hit the gas
pedal and spun the car around. As they sped off, the man in the
front passenger seat tried to shoot at the beast with Matlock's gun.
However, the gun wouldn't fire.

The next day Wilson and Matlock returned to the scene
where they found footprints. "I put my arm down in one of the
prints," Matlock said, "and that print was as long as from my elbow to the tip of my outstretched fingers."

Another sighting in proximity to the South Sulphur River
occurred in August 1978. As documented in the same *FATE* article, High School Senior, Harvey Garrison, was driving along a

country road at about 10:15 p.m. when he saw what appeared to be a seven-foot-tall creature standing by the side of the road.

"I slammed on my brakes and came within a few feet of hitting the thing," he told investigators. "It turned slightly toward my car. Then in one step it was across the road!" [56] It disappeared into the blackness of the night.

Two days later, three more teenagers from the small community of South Sulphur were reportedly frightened by a similar beast while walking on the very same road at midnight. Upon hearing something moving in the trees, they walked over to investigate when a large animal jumped up and ran away. They described it as being larger than a gorilla and "well over seven feet tall."

Following the incident, one of the teenagers, Wayne Matlock (no apparent relationship to the previously mentioned Jerry Matlock) saw the alleged beast a second time. On or around August 19, Wayne was walking home along another rural road at 5:00 p.m. when a creature fitting the same description ran out of the woods and headed for the river.

"It crossed the road several yards in front of me and headed off across a pasture toward the Middle Sulphur River," he told investigators. "The cattle in the pasture went running in all directions and cattle usually run together in the same direction unless they're really scared."

Matlock said he was so startled he ran the rest of the way home. He and one of the other boys eventually returned to the site to look for evidence. They claimed to have found two footprints in a ditch at the side of the road. "Each one was over 12 inches long," he stated.

Matlock's father, Harold, went on record saying that he believed the boy's story. He theorized that "the creature could be migrating along the rivers from some other area, such as Boggy Creek in Arkansas," where a string of highly publicized sightings had taken place in 1971.

In 1977, a man was driving toward Commerce at around 11:00 p.m. when he noticed movement on the side of the road as he approached the Sulphur River Bottoms. As he got closer, a "very large animal" ran across the road "upright, but just slightly slumped forward as it moved." It had a very long stride. Another car saw it as well and braked to get a better look. The animal disappeared quickly into the deep shadows surrounding the bottoms as the witness continued down the highway.[57]

In October 1984, a woman had a rather startling encounter along a small tributary of the Sulphur River called Anderson Creek. The witness said she was walking along the creek in Bowie County one evening at dusk when she began to hear the sound of footsteps in the leaves as a rank smell entered her nostrils. Looking toward the sound, she saw something standing by the edge of the water. It had rained earlier in the day, leaving a light fog hanging in the air, but there was still enough visibility to see that it was not human.

The thing, she recalled, was approximately seven feet tall with a body covered in black hair. It had long arms that hung down almost to its knees. In the foggy dusk it was hard to make out facial details, but she was certain it had no visible ears atop its head, which would indicate a bear. Frightened, the witness turned and ran as fast as she could back home, never looking back to see if the creature was following.

"I have never been as scared as I was in that moment," she reported. "I remember seeing it breathe. It was completely motionless except for the slight movement as it breathed in and out, and that is what frightened me so very bad, because I knew that it was real and I was not just seeing something among the trees."[58]

Perhaps something unknown had been living in the Anderson Creek bottoms for years. According to local rumors, a farmer allegedly found strange tracks near his well in the 1940s.

In 1985, Donald Rucker and his father were traveling on a farm road near the Sulphur River Bottoms in Hunt County at around 8:00 p.m. when they spotted what looked like a light coming over the railroad tracks about a half mile ahead. As they got closer, they realized it was actually their headlights reflecting off a huge animal standing beside the road. It stood upright and had long, silvery white hair that gleamed in the light.

"The animal started to move from the left side to the right side of the road as I got closer," Rucker reported to the Texas Bigfoot Research Center. "I was about fifty feet from the animal when it crossed the road to the right side."[59]

The men were too scared to stop and investigate, so they drove on. Rucker said a few weeks later he was talking to a couple of friends who mentioned they saw the very same animal a week or so after Rucker and his father saw it.

In the adjacent county of Delta, a witness had a very similar sighting in 1992. He was driving near the Sulphur River at around midnight when he saw a "dark colored, upright figure, like a big man dart across the road."[60] He only caught a glimpse in his high beams but was sure it wasn't an actual person. The stretch of road is remote, dark, and flanked by heavy woods on either side.

The area of the Sulphur River Bottoms in Delta County near Jim Chapman Lake (also known as Cooper Lake) seems to be a hot spot with a long history of strange reports. Folks in the area as far back as the 1940s spoke of a creature they called the "nude woman."[61] It was described as some kind of large, upright animal that was occasionally seen along the edge of the wood line but never coming out into the open. No one was actually sure it was a woman, but that was the name it was given. The oddly named animal might have existed purely in legend if not for modern-day sightings.

In the fall of 1995, a man was trudging through a Delta County pecan thicket at night looking for a rogue cow when his flashlight beam landed on a hairy beast he believed to be the creature that had long been seen in the area. According to the witness, his son-in-law had previously encountered a Bigfoot-like animal in the river bottoms near Cooper Lake.

In 2015, the editor of a small Delta County newspaper called the *Cooper Review* was confronted by what is normally a tongue-in-cheek affair for most journalists. In the October 29, 2015 issue, Cindy Roller recounted the startling experience. Roller said she had just left the newspaper office and was driving home as she normally did.

> *Motoring my way out to Farm-to-Market 154 with the sun starting to set in my rearview mirror I noticed there wasn't much traffic as I stopped at the curve that meets State Highway 19. With no one approaching I get up to the speed limited as I come around the curve near the bridge over the Sulphur River. All of a sudden in my headlights something tall and hairy raced across my path. It was about five feet in front of me. I lost sight of it as it entered the field to the west of me. It went so fast I didn't even have time to react. No time to hit the brakes. No time to even reach for my cell phone. Was it Bigfoot? Chills came over my entire body.*[62]

A few days later Roller was talking to a Texas Department of Public Safety trooper about some other matters when she decided to tell him about the strange experience. When asked if he'd heard of any unusual sightings in the area lately, the trooper told her a kangaroo had been on the loose in Delta County. A *kangaroo*?! The officer was serious, though he did not have an explanation as to how or why the animal was roaming the area.

Roller considered the possibility of a kangaroo, but the animal she saw seemed far too fast and agile to be a hopping marsupial. "Unfortunately he didn't have many answers for me and probably now thinks I am one keystroke shy of sane, too," she wrote, humorously. "But I know what I saw. It was too tall to be a deer, too fast to be a human."

It's a statement all too familiar in the realms of Bigfoot lore.

The Sulphur River
(Photo by Lyle Blackburn)

Beasts Beyond the Lake

As we travel further east along the Sulphur River, where the multiple branches now merge into a single, strong path, we find yet more locations where people have reported man-like beasts. One of these areas is Wright Patman Lake, a Sulphur River flood control reservoir originally known as "Lake Texarkana." Tales of wood apes here date back to at least 1916, when a family living in a place called Knight's Bluff,[vi] west of Queen City, saw a strange, ape-like thing near their country home.

According to a woman who was a young girl at the time, her family was traveling home late one night in a mule-drawn wagon when they heard a strange noise coming from across their pasture; something like an eerie, high-pitched wail or howl. Their mules heaved nervously as the family looked across the moonlit field to see what had made the noise. After a few moments, they saw a tall figure emerge from a line of trees and walk into the moonlight. The woman described it as being "tall or taller than a man and covered with long, dark hair." She also noted "it stood absolutely erect and walked slowly toward them like a man . . . not slouching like an ape." The creature advanced across the field toward the wagon as it continued to howl, all the while motioning angrily with its long arms. The father grabbed a rifle and fired at the creature. It was enough to send it running back into the woods.[63]

Encounters in the area continue to be reported today. John Swatha, a resident of Argo, Texas, told me he was hiking around Wright Patman Lake in the late 1970s when he heard some movement in the trees like someone walking toward him. After a few moments, he could see a tall, upright animal behind some trees some thirty yards away. It appeared to be standing on two legs

---

vi Today there is still a campground on the edge of Wright Patman Lake called Knight's Bluff, but the original Knight's Bluff community was covered by water when the lake was created by the U.S. Army Corps of Engineers in 1953.

with "a pointed head" and covered in "nearly black hair about three to four inches in length." The animal paused when it spotted Swatha and then quickly darted away in the other direction. It was upright the entire time.

An eerily identical report was filed with the Texas Bigfoot Research Center. In this case the witness said that in November 1986 his nephew had joined him for an evening of hunting near Maud on the west side of Wright Patman. They had been in different tree stands, so just before it got dark, the man climbed down from his and started heading to the stand where his nephew was hunting. In his own words:

> *I started up a creek bottom that ran into a big swamp thicket next to the lake when I smelled something with a very foul odor. I could hear something moving in the thicket, at first I thought it might be a deer, but it was too big to be a deer, and sounded more like a man walking in the water, so then I thought my nephew had got down and started to my stand. I yelled his name so he would know I was coming his way. This thing started moving away from me fast. Down the thicket about 50 to 75 yards there was an opening about 30 feet across, [and] this thing crossed the opening. I could not believe what I was seeing. This thing was around 6 to 7 feet tall with dark brown hair covering its whole body. It crossed the opening in what seemed to be 5 or 6 steps! I'm not crazy, I know I saw something and whatever this thing was it was BIG.[64]*

In October 1990, five witnesses (!) watched a hairy, man-like thing run across the road near Atlanta, south of Wright Patman. It was around midnight when a woman, her friend, and her three children were driving along Highway 59. Suddenly, one of them screamed out "What is that?!" A large, hairy, upright figure had bolted onto the highway in front of the vehicle. It was so close the driver and the others could clearly see it.

"It was tall and hairy like a bear, but it was running quickly across the road," the primary witness reported to the Texas Bigfoot Research Conservancy (TBRC).[vii] "When it got to the other side it stopped for a second then ran into the woods."[65]

Investigator Daryl Colyer followed up and interviewed several of the witnesses. They estimated the thing's height at "no less than seven feet" and agreed that it was covered with hair, much like a gorilla or chimpanzee. The witnesses were certain it moved on two legs the entire time, swinging its arms and moving in a smooth motion. They were not familiar with the concept of Bigfoot at the time, so they were completely baffled. It was not until years later that they realized it could have been a Bigfoot. In terms of a possible hoax or misidentification, Colyer did not believe that was the case. "All witnesses had clear recollection of an upright and tall subject," Colyer writes. "There is no other species that can be comfortably applied within such descriptive parameters. I could detect no hints or signs of hoaxing, either by the witnesses or that they were hoaxed. It seems unlikely that someone larger than the average human would don a suit and risk running across Highway 59 only a few car lengths in front of a vehicle traveling at approximately 60 miles per hour; while possible, it seems improbable."[66]

I certainly agree with his assessment.

Several years ago, I was contacted by Jami Longacre, who lives with her husband in the very same countryside in Atlanta, Texas. She told me of several alarming incidents. The first occurred in July 2012 when they heard an eerie, scream-like roar coming from the woods one evening at around 10:30 p.m. They had never

---

vii The Texas Bigfoot Research Center, founded in 1999, transitioned to the Texas Bigfoot Research Conservancy in 2007 and later became the North American Wood Ape Conservancy in 2013. Throughout this work, the name used will reflect the name of the organization at the time of each report.

heard anything like it.

Later, around midnight, they were preparing for bed when they heard three booming whoops outside the house. The noise was so loud, it sounded as if the animal—or whatever had made the sound—was standing right outside their bedroom window. "It scared us so bad, the hair on the back of our necks actually stood up," she told me.

After a few moments without any further sounds, Jami's husband went to the front door, slowly opened it, and looked out. He did not see anything out of the ordinary, but could smell a pungent odor, as if a wild animal had been there moments before. He quickly closed and locked the door.

A short time later, the couple relaxed enough to venture outside to have a better look around. Again, they did not see anything strange, but they did hear another screaming whoop deeper in the woods to the west. It made them feel better knowing the thing had apparently moved on.

By February 2013, Jami had all but forgotten the spooky incident as she and a coworker drove home from their night-shift job. As Jami slowed to turn onto her county road, she glanced over to see a tall animal standing in the ditch beside it. The ditch was at least five feet deep, yet she could still see part of its huge mass above the ditch line, touching the low-hanging branches of the tree above it. It looked to be reddish brown in color.

Her friend saw the startled look on her face and asked what was the matter. Before she could reply, the figure ran behind the car and disappeared into the blackness. She couldn't make out details of its shape in her rearview mirror, but she was sure it ran behind them because it flashed across the reflectors mounted on the neighbor's mailbox.

"I don't know if it was Bigfoot, but I know it was huge," she said. "And it scared me to death."

As the Sulphur River continues east from Wright Patman Lake on its path to join the Red River, sightings continue all the way to the edge of Texas and beyond as the waters cross into Arkansas. It is here that I investigated one of the most convincing encounters I've come across to date. Not only was the witness in this case credible, but she was able to view the creature at close range in the clear light of day.

The woman (who asked to remain anonymous) said she was driving away from her home on the north side of the Sulphur River at around 10:00 a.m. on November 24, 2014, when she realized she had forgotten something. As she completed a three-point turn on the narrow county thoroughfare and began to head back south, she was startled to see something standing in the middle of the road. At first she thought it was a kid dressed in a Halloween costume, but as she focused on the figure, she realized it was some sort of hairy animal standing on two legs.

The creature had apparently come out of the thick patch of woods on her left and was crossing the road where her car had been moments before. Now that she had turned around, it paused as if caught in the act. The creature stood fully upright with an estimated height of five feet. It was covered in reddish-brown hair, except for the face, which had dark, leathery skin and piercing eyes. She could see the wispy hair on its arms waving in the gentle morning breeze. It gazed at the woman for a few seconds before turning and running back into the woods.

As she recounted the story in person to myself and my late research partner, Tom Shirley, we could hear the emotion in her voice. We watched the earnest expression in her eyes. It was apparent that feelings of fear and bewilderment still lingered. "It scared me to death," she told us.

I asked her if there was any possibility it could have been a person in a costume, perhaps trying to scare passersby. "The more I looked at it, I could see it wasn't," she explained. "When it was running, it didn't look like a costume—it looked like a real animal."

Tom and I visited the location where she said the creature entered the road. The thick woods standing to the east were indeed a likely place for an animal to emerge. There were a few houses in the vicinity, but it was a very rural setting with the houses far apart and mostly nestled into the trees. A large, open field sat on the opposite side of the road, presumably where the creature was headed. I wasn't sure why it would want to cross into such an open area in the light of day, but regardless, if a large animal were to move around there, this seemed like the most likely place.

As Tom and I took a few photos and poked around in the woods just off the road, inevitably a resident drove up and questioned our intentions. The person was initially suspicious, but after I explained who I was, it led to a phone conversation with the person who owned the wooded property. When I told him a woman had claimed to see a Bigfoot-like creature cross the road there, he was intrigued. He wasn't aware of any other reports from his neighbors, but he did tell me that aside from a few houses, the woods basically ran unimpeded for miles in the direction of Fouke.

I also asked him if it was possible some kids in the area had dressed up in a Bigfoot costume in the days preceding Thanksgiving. He told me there were no kids other than his own that lived along that stretch of road, and that it was highly unlikely. He also pointed out that kids would have been in school the morning of Monday, November 24.

Considering all the information, it seemed as though the woman had a legitimate encounter, which is not only significant in regard to its probability, but also in its proximity to the river. To those that have read my book, *The Beast of Boggy Creek: The True Story of the Fouke Monster*, the significance of the Sulphur River is apparent. If you haven't read my book (yet), then suffice to say that numerous sightings of the legendary creature made famous by the 1972 movie, *The Legend of Boggy Creek*, occurred along its banks and in the swampy bottomlands surrounding it. Given this, it would not be out of the question for such creatures to travel up and down the riverway searching for food or higher ground during times of flooding. The fact that Boggy Creek Monster sightings are not simply confined within the borders of Arkansas, but extend well into Texas along the waterway, seems to support the credibility of not only the Boggy Creek creature but those of the Lone Star Bigfoot. As waterways such as the Sulphur River and the Red River meander across the countryside, they always bring with them an air of mystery that flows directly to the heart of the Bigfoot phenomenon.

Location where the witness encountered a strange creature on November 24, 2014

(Photo by Lyle Blackburn)

4.

CROSS TIMBERS CREATURES

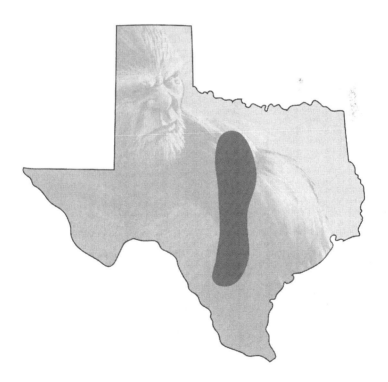

While the majority of modern Texas Bigfoot sightings come from the eastern third of the state, there are some highly compelling reports that originate from the central portion. These are typically found within the Cross Timbers and Blackland Prairies ecological regions where a mosaic of forest, woodland, savanna, and prairies offer a striking transition between the Piney Woods of the east and the High Plains of the west. Some of these locations are not what we would consider typical Bigfoot habitat, yet there are sufficient waterways and flourishing tree cover that could offer such creatures a reasonable terrain and respite from the glaring eye of the sun. Just as the early explorers of Texas may have faced challenges here, one would only need to travel a relatively short distance within these areas to find alternate terrains more appropriate for survival. Perhaps this is the case with any such wayward beasts traversing the wilds of mid-Texas.

Brazos Ape-Man

When I was young, my father had a bowhunting lease at Possum Kingdom, a lake and state park area west of Fort Worth. As far back as I can remember, we spent every weekend during deer season camped on the property along with several of my father's work friends who also hunted. The area is a great slice of Texas landscape with a mix of gnarly mesquites, grassy flats, and craggy hills that twist in and around the winding Possum Kingdom Lake and its source tributary, the Brazos River.

I can remember spending hours sitting next to my father in tree stands that were nothing more than a weathered two-by-six nailed precariously between some branches. I was around six years old when I started hunting with him, so it was always a challenge to sit still for that long, especially on an uncomfortable board. But I really didn't mind. I would anxiously watch the spot where he had put out deer corn waiting for a big buck to creep in. If I was lucky, I'd get to see a fox or bobcat. I didn't really care if we got a deer or not. It was always exhilarating to be out in the middle of nowhere observing wildlife that, for the most part, never realized we were there. In those years at the lease, it never even occurred to me that we might see a Bigfoot!

The author as a boy (left) bowhunting with his father, Joe (right)

I didn't discover tales of Sasquatch until I was in third grade, and when I did, it was stories from the Pacific Northwest. Had I known there was a chance to see a Bigfoot in Texas, I'm not sure if it would have made me more excited or just plain fearful. It's one thing to see a huge buck in the wild standing twenty yards away, but to see a seven-foot-tall, ape-like thing walk under our crude tree stand would be absolutely shocking. What would it do if it saw us? Would it simply walk on, or would it come closer and observe us? Or would it try to attack us? I can only imagine what would have happened if one would have approached. But I didn't have to worry about that, right? Bigfoots didn't live in Texas. And if they did, surely they wouldn't be anywhere near the craggy hills of Possum Kingdom. Wrong. Apparently, very wrong. Legends of ape-like creatures lurking in the area date back far enough that they *are* legends. And whispers of something the locals call the Brazos Ape-Man may prove to be more than just a legend.

Palo Pinto County, where Possum Kingdom is located, has racked up a fair amount of strange sightings over the years that sound very much like classic Bigfoot. One of the oldest reports comes from 1969. According to the witness, he was at a summer camp in the area when he was fourteen years old. He and about twenty other campers and two counselors had set out on an extended canoe/camping excursion down the Brazos River. They put in just below the dam at Possum Kingdom Lake.

"The first night we camped near and before the Highway 4 bridge," the witness said. "As we were setting up camp and securing the canoes for the night, several campers noticed some type of unknown animal peering down on us from the cliff."[67]

They could only see glimpses of its head, so it was hard to identify. Eventually it went away, and they spent the rest of the night sleeping in their tents. The next morning the boys were talking about what kind of animal it might have been. One boy believed it might have been a fox. Curious, the boys decided to make a quick climb up the cliff face to see if they could see anything. In his own words:

> I had found a way to get up the cliff face and we were on top in no time. As we made the last push to the top, we could hear something running off through the woods. We immediately gave chase and I was in the lead. There were some very large boulders scattered about and I ran around one of the larger ones. As I came flying around the edge of this boulder, I ran smack into a rather large "tree," which

knocked me back flat on my rump. I was crumpled at the base of this tree and dazed. When my eyes focused again, I noticed the tree had hair! I looked up, it screamed, I peed in my pants (literally), my friend screamed, I screamed, it screamed again, and all of this in quick but distorted time. We ran fast and right off the edge of the cliff. We were in a blind panic.

What the witness first took to be a tree was a huge, upright creature covered in dark hair. When he ran into it, the witness was looking straight ahead, and he was seeing the animal from the waist down. After he looked up, he realized what it was. When the thing screamed, the sound was so loud the witness said he could literally feel a vibration through his body. He and one other boy got a good look at the creature before it ran off.

When the boys descended the cliff and returned to camp, they explained to the counselors what they had seen. Everyone in camp had heard the commotion, but no one believed they had encountered such a beast.

"At the time, no one around there had even heard of a Bigfoot, so it was hard to explain," the witness continued. "We said it was a giant gorilla, but that didn't go over too well with anybody, including the other campers and counselors who heard the screams and witnessed our fall, from grace as it turned out—they thought we were crazy and made the whole thing up."

It seemed like an unlikely place and an unlikely way to encounter such a creature, but there was no doubt in the young man's mind what he and his friend had run into. This was in clear daylight, and there could be no mix-up with a common animal such as a fox or anything else native to the Brazos River corridor. The witness mentioned hearing legends of what was called the Brazos Ape-Man or, even more bizarrely, Hugo's Monster. He could only assume that he himself had run headlong into one of these legends.

A decade later, another incident involved a troop of Boys Scouts, young campers not much different from me. According to a report submitted to the Texas Bigfoot Research Center, the troop was camped at the Worth Ranch Boy Scout reservation near Possum Kingdom in 1978, when they got the shock of their life. It was around midnight and several of the boys were returning to camp from a Scout ceremony. Suddenly, a figure emerged from the trees and crossed the road in front of their truck. It was very tall and upright on two legs.

"We could see it very clearly," the witness (now grown) recalled. "It was black, its arms were very long, and its head was almost conical."

The thing walked into the trees and disappeared into the darkness. The witness estimated that it had to be around nine feet tall, judging from measurements they took of the nearby tree the next day.

Another boy had seen something similar the night before. "A friend of mine said he saw something run behind a building that was located in the bottoms, and that it was human-like," the witness explained. "It scared the hell out of him."

The former Boy Scout spent seven years camping in the area and during that time heard rumors that some of the workers at Worth Ranch had also reported several strange encounters, but he could never get any direct information from them. He was, however, able to recount an incident that happened to his room-mate in 1981 while they were living in Mineral Wells. One evening the roommate and his girlfriend came home in an obvious state of distress. When asked what was going on, the young man said he and his girl were parking at a spot on the Brazos River when they saw something very disturbing.

"I was at home when he and his girlfriend showed up, both looked like they had just seen a ghost," he recalled. "They told me they were parked near the road and were in the backseat when she saw something moving outside the car. My friend jumped up and turned around to see a large, hairy ape-like creature standing next to the car just looking at them. He said he didn't even stop to put on his pants as he jumped over the seat, started the car and headed out fast."[68] The roommate couldn't say it was definitely a "Bigfoot," but when placed in context to the other alleged sightings, it seems like a possibility.

If I was doubtful of any such occurrences in the Possum Kingdom area, my skepticism was waylaid by something that happened to one of my own friends when he was a Boy Scout camping in the very same area! My longtime friend and former bandmate, Lee Lynch, said he was at the Worth Ranch Boy Scout Camp the very same year (1981) when they embarked on a day hike. In his own words:

> I was with a few other scouts, and we were going toward a small outcropping known as "Hugo's Mountain." We were traveling on a slight upgrade on the trail leading to the mountain, and as we crossed a dried mud bank where runoff occurs, I was looking down to watch my step, and noticed a series of impressions in the mud. They crossed the path and seemed to follow the mud bank for a short distance. I noticed huge footprints alternating with what were apparently large fist prints dried into the mud.

> The prints were human-like, but much larger than average. A conservative estimate would be fourteen inches length on the foot, and six inches width on the fist. The feet were abnormally wide for a human, and the smaller toes seemed curled more than normal. The definition of the knuckles and pores of the fist prints was, in some areas, quite clear. The flesh prints on the toe areas were quite clearly imprinted into the mud. The creases in the foot where skin naturally folds were apparent.

From the look of the stride, the human or humanoid had been steadying itself with fists as it moved through wet mud. Each print had sliding tracks from the center of gravity.

We went to get a Scout leader, and a warden was called. They roped the area off and were studying the prints. We hung around for a few minutes eager to see what they had to say, but they were reluctant to give details, and we had to report back to camp for scheduled events.[69]

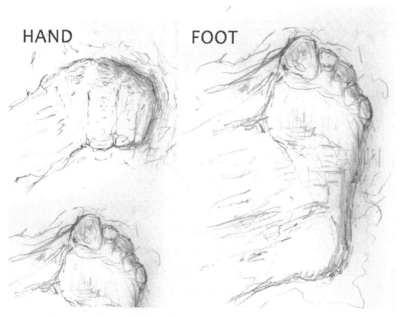

HAND FOOT

Illustration by Lee Lynch depicting the handprint
and footprints he observed in Palo Pinto County

Unfortunately Lee never heard any other details or conclusions from the Scout leaders. It was a mystery that has hung with him for all these years. It wasn't until later, as we discussed the possibility of Bigfoot in Texas, that it made any sort of sense. He doesn't recall anyone reporting a visual encounter, but the presence of the strange footprints in the mud cannot be disputed.

Hugo's Monster

The origin of the term "Brazos Ape-Man" is obvious since the creature seen around the northern section of the Brazos River was essentially a human-like ape. The origin of the alternate moniker, "Hugo's Monster," is more interesting. According to a campfire tale told in the Palo Pinto area, in the early 1900s there was a man named Hugo who had graduated from medical school somewhere up North. He would have been a successful doctor if not for his obsession with trying to perfect the grafting of body parts. He started by experimenting on animals, trying to attach new legs and then later transplanting kidneys, eyes, and even hearts.

When the local citizens learned of the morbid experiments, they literally ran him out of town. Hugo fled and eventually ended up in Palo Pinto, where he set up a laboratory inside a cave on Kyle Mountain (the largest peak in the area). There he become obsessed with the rather Frankenstein-influenced objective to transplant a human brain. In the subsequent months, Hugo supposedly received huge, wooden shipping crates by way of train. This caught the attention of the local sheriff, but all attempts to see what was inside of the crates failed.

Eventually, the daughter of a local rancher went missing, and the trail led authorities to Hugo's mountain cave. There they found a horrific, blood-covered scene. Hugo was covered in blood after having just completed a crude operation in which he transplanted the brain of the (now deceased) girl into a live gorilla! The gorilla, obviously brought in by one of the mysterious crates, was now resting in a cage. The lawmen ordered Hugo to surrender, but he merely laughed and informed them that the whole lab was rigged with dynamite. The sheriff shot Hugo, but he still managed to blow up the place. Hugo was presumably killed, while the gorilla escaped. It was later seen roaming the hills near Kyle Mountain, and from then on, people would occasionally see it, giving rise to the ape sightings in the area.

This legend is obviously outlandish and surely untrue, but it does prompt the question as to whether the story was concocted to explain the various sightings of a large, ape-like creature in the area or whether the story influenced people to believe there was an ape-like creature in the area. Either way, there is a significant history of some fairly credible sightings in the area, which suggests there may be something to the stories.

In retrospect, I wish I would have known about Bigfoot in Texas or the legend of "Hugo's Monster" back in the days I hunted Possum Kingdom as a kid. I surely would have looked at the area differently and perhaps would have found a footprint or two myself.

They Always Travel the Creeks

While researching Bigfoot sightings in a particular area, I often come across reports in the outlying vicinity that seem to corroborate the presence of a large, unknown creature (or creatures) perhaps roaming a wider area during the very same time period. Shortly after looking into the Palo Pinto stories, I spoke to Gino Napoli, who told me of several unnerving incidents that happened in Parker County a mere thirty miles east. These encounters seem eerily similar to the reports by the Boy Scouts and others.

Napoli told me he was parked in a secluded backwoods area with his girlfriend in 1981 when they experienced a strange sighting. They were in high school at the time, so they often drove to a wooded area near Town Creek for privacy. On this particular night, Napoli and his girlfriend were in her car—doing what young folks do in private settings—while some of his buddies were parked in a truck nearby with their own girlfriends.

"We were in the backseat with the windows cracked when I heard something walking up to the car," Napoli told me. "I thought it was a human being because it was on two legs."

Napoli's girlfriend was immediately alarmed and asked him what it was. Napoli couldn't see anything yet, but his first thought was that it might be a hobo. There was a railroad track close by, so perhaps the person was a vagrant train hopper.

"Of course we were kids, so I'm thinking he's gonna kill us and take the car," Napoli quipped.

The thought of a person approaching them in the dark was alarming enough, but to make things even spookier, they noticed that the woods had gone completely silent. There was an owl that had been hooting from a nearby tree, but it had suddenly stopped. The bugs and frogs had also suspended their nightly chorus, as if they sensed something unnatural.

At that point, Napoli was so spooked, he jumped into the front seat and started up the car. "I started the car up and threw it in reverse," he explained. "I floored it and backed up and I finally found the headlights. As I was going backward and turning, the headlights went across the woods."

There, in the stark light of the beam, Napoli and his girlfriend saw a huge figure run between the trees, headed in the direction of the creek. The thing was tall with wide shoulders and had virtually no neck. They were not sure what it was, except it was not a person, hobo or otherwise.

Napoli drove the car down the narrow dirt road, stopping briefly at his buddy's truck as they fled. He was shocked to learn they had also seen something run by their vehicle. He then raced to his girlfriend's house, where he dropped her off before going home to get a gun and a light. His brother was home at the time, so he told him what had happened.

The Napoli brothers grabbed their handguns and a battery-powered Q-Beam light and drove back to the woods, where they rejoined Gino's two friends. The four of them proceeded to search the area for signs. It wasn't long before they found sliding footprint tracks in the mud where the thing must have crossed the creek. The tracks were not very defined because of the muddy substrate but were clear enough to show that something big had indeed been running on two legs from the area where they had been parked. The tracks disappeared into the thick leaves of the woods.

As they continued to look around, Napoli noticed that once again the woods became eerily silent. Suddenly they heard a branch break. They shined the light ahead, fully expecting to see something emerge from the trees. After a few tense minutes, however, nothing came into view as the insects and frogs resumed their chatter. The boys eventually left the woods, coming away with more questions than answers about what might have been living out there.

The Napolis continued to search the area from time to time, but only saw something notable on one other occasion when Gino's brother caught a glimpse of a huge, hairy thing moving among the trees after they heard a noisy ruckus and scream from the brush. He didn't get a good enough look at it, however, to confirm just what it was.

As Napoli shared his story with others, he was shocked to learn of more sightings. In one case, a young man named Ricky, whom he met through a paintball tournament, said he had seen something twice along the same creek. Ricky said that on one occasion, he was headed down to fix a fence on his aunt's dairy farm, riding a horse and pulling a pack horse behind. Suddenly both horses began to jitter and buck nervously as if something up ahead was scaring them. The pack horse was so agitated, it broke loose and took off in the opposite direction. As Ricky tried to calm his own horse, he looked ahead to see what was causing the panic. He then saw a large, upright, hairy creature moving in the trees a short distance away. It quickly disappeared from view in the shadowy woods. He had heard stories about such a creature from some of the adults in the area, but until then had not put much stock in the tales.

Sometime later, Ricky had taken his girlfriend fishing down in the creek. They were walking along the bank when they noticed a very foul odor. Ricky wasn't sure what it was, so they continued to walk. As they rounded a bend they were shocked to see a hairy, man-like thing down on one knee drinking from the creek. It looked up and saw them at about the same time they saw it. Ricky said they turned and fled as the creature got up and ran the other direction down the creek. It appeared to be the very same animal he had seen previously while riding his horse.

While Napoli had no way of knowing if Ricky's story was true, a chance meeting with his ex-girlfriend six months later would give him a solid indication that it was. Napoli and his friends were having a party when a group of girls showed up. Napoli knew one of them, but not the others. At some point they were sitting around talking about ghosts and Bigfoot when one of the girls said she had once seen a Bigfoot. As she told the story, Napoli was utterly amazed. It turns out she was the one dating Ricky at the time and had been with him when they saw the thing drinking from the creek.

It seems that corroboration can come in unexpected ways, just as unexpected as the encounters themselves. The fact that these incidents occurred in the same general time frame as the ones in the adjacent Palo Pinto County makes them all the more intriguing.

The tangled woods of Central Texas
(Photo by Lyle Blackburn)

San Antonio Anthropoids

Directly south across the Cross Timbers, at the tip of the Blackland Prairies region, lies the Texas city of San Antonio. Here, one can find the famous site of the Alamo, as well as the Riverwalk, a mecca of romantic sidewalks and restaurants built twelve feet below the street along the route of the San Antonio River. One may also find . . . Bigfoot?

As one of the largest cities in Texas, San Antonio may seem unlikely for a Bigfoot sighting, but there have been some instances where strange creatures were spotted in the pockets of woodlands surrounding the outlying areas, and in one case, surprisingly close to the city.

According to the classic *Bigfoot Casebook*, a man named

John Martinez and his friend, Rick, were hunting rabbits on the outskirts of San Antonio in November 1974 when they came upon a six-to-seven-foot-tall "Bigfoot with long, matted hair on its head."[70]

In 1976, *The San Antonio Light* newspaper reported that another creature had been seen near the Kelly Air Force Base. A few weeks before September 1st, Ed Olivarri was preparing for work one morning when his dog began barking wildly in the backyard. Concerned, he went to investigate. As he looked over his back fence toward the woods, a train whistle sounded from a nearby railroad track.

"The animal must have been hiding or lying down because when the whistle blew it started running," Olivarri told reporters. "It looked like it was some kind of 'Big Foot' monster." He said it was "about seven feet tall with short brown hair over its body" and definitely ran on two legs.[71]

On August 30, Olivarri's next-door neighbor, Rosa Medina, claimed to have seen a similar yet smaller bipedal animal, which was perhaps a juvenile Bigfoot. When her dog began barking at about 3:00 a.m., she went to her back window to investigate. In the glow of a security light, she could see an animal with light-brown fur sitting on her back step.[72] It was distinctly "ape-like" and about the size of a child.

Medina was too frightened to open the door, so she tapped on the windowpane. Upon hearing the noise, the animal jumped up and ran off on two feet. Medina estimated its height to be approximately three feet.

When Olivarri heard about his neighbor's sighting, he decided to search the woods behind their houses. There he discovered large, foot-like impressions along a creek bank. A game warden was summoned to analyze the suspected tracks, but unfortunately they were trampled by reporters and other curious people who converged on the location. Authorities could find no explanation for the events.

Even today, Bigfoot-like creatures have been reported there. A woman had the scare of her life when she saw a tall, hairy thing watching her as she was working in a construction office trailer in the spring of 2005. According to a report filed with the Bigfoot Field Researchers Organization, the woman and her husband had been contracted to clean model homes in a new housing development on the edge of San Antonio. As part of that service, they cleaned a trailer that was used as an office for the construction workers. It was located at the back of the development at the bottom of a hill near the woods. One night as the woman was carrying cleaning supplies out of the trailer, she looked to her right and saw a "tall, hairy figure with a pointed head watching her from behind a tree."[73] It was fairly close, perhaps twenty-five yards away. The woman stood still and observed the figure for several minutes as it leaned around the tree watching her. Finally she became so spooked she ran back inside and told her husband. The husband immediately turned off the lights in the trailer and went outside to have a look. He did not see anything but knew his wife had not been making up the story.

On two previous occasions, something had banged on the side of the trailer, but when they looked out, they saw nothing. They had also heard strange whistling sounds coming from the nearby woods that didn't seem like birds.

Shaken, the couple quickly packed up and ran to their car. They turned on the headlights so they could see into the woods, but again the watcher was nowhere to be seen. The woman estimated its height to be at least seven feet, with its stocky body weighing perhaps three hundred fifty pounds or more. It was covered in shaggy hair that appeared to be black in color. She never saw it again but felt certain that whatever she saw was not a normal animal.

In November 2009, news of a bizarre 911 call made local

headlines. In the call, a homeless woman named Jennifer (calling from a cell phone[viii]) claimed she and her husband saw a "creepy scary very large creature devour a deer and run off clear across the road."[74] The call, which was made public, began:

> **911 Dispatch**: *911 San Antonio. Do you need Police Fire or EMS?*

> **Caller**: *I'm not real sure ma'am. Um, I just watched the biggest creat-- critter, but it smelled real bad. I'm a homeless female, I live right in the middle of the woods around 151 and Culebra. Just north where the light is. This thing was seventy-five feet away from me, smelled awful, devoured a deer carcass and then took off and like screamed, screeched; and took off across the street. And I know you guys are going to think I'm crazy, but I'm dead serious, there was something very big. Bigger—a lot bigger than me—out here. So we thought it was something you should know.*

Jennifer and her husband lived in a tent in a wooded area on the west side of San Antonio near the TX-1604 Loop. The area was frequented by homeless people who would use it as a camp. During the call, Jennifer went on to explain that the thing appeared to be at least six feet tall and was covered with fur or hair. They watched it pick up the deer carcass and run from the area, breaking branches as it let out a blood-curdling howl. She estimated it had been standing no more than thirty feet away when she first caught sight of it. It was a dark, rainy night, but she had no doubt as to what she saw. Jennifer never used the word "Bigfoot," but her description fits firmly in the category.

The woman and her husband seemed absolutely sincere, lucid, and genuinely scared. The official police report noted that

---

viii It may seem odd that a homeless person has a cell phone, but sometimes they do.

she "did not sound intoxicated."[75] An officer was dispatched to the area and instructed to sound his siren when he arrived so Jennifer could meet him at the road. He did so, but Jennifer never emerged from the woods, and the officer eventually left. In a subsequent interview, she explained that she did not come out to meet the officer because it would have required her to walk through the dark woods.[76] She was simply too frightened, fearing the creature could still be out there.

The police did not return to examine the scene, however, the following day, cryptozoologist Ken Gerhard (who resides in San Antonio) went to the scene along with local television news reporter, Joe Conger. Gerhard did a search of the general area but found no conclusive evidence of an unusual creature.

A short time later, author and Bigfoot investigator, Michael Mayes, was able to obtain Jennifer's cell phone number (via a friend who located the 911 call transcript) and gave her a call. The woman was more than willing to share more details. In his Texas Cryptid Hunter blog, Mayes notes that Jennifer told him she had been walking near a clothesline hung up in their campsite when "she noticed a large hair-covered upright creature staring at her from the other side of the line."[77] She looked at it a few moments before it bolted away, picked up a deer carcass, and disappeared into the brush. It made a loud, screaming noise as it ran. She said the noise was like no sound she or her husband had ever heard before. It was dark, but the thing was very close to the camp where they had a big fire that gave off sufficient light.

She described the animal as "dark and covered in hair or fur," between seven and eight feet tall, and upright on two legs the entire time. It was able to pick up the deer carcass (which had not been there previously) with very little effort. She said the animal "tucked [the deer] under its arm like a football."

Jennifer explained the event in detail as her husband talked in the background, corroborating the story. She seemed sincere and convincing, although after telling Mayes about the encounter she told him she believed that ever since the 911 call that "government vehicles" had been driving around the area, as if they were doing some kind of surveillance. She claimed to have heard a "very high frequency sound come from the vehicles during their extended stays" as if they were trying to flush the creature out of hiding. She also felt that a family of creatures may be in the area and that they were trying to "communicate with her by thinking." In light of these bizarre claims, it raises some red flags about her overall credibility. Many have theorized that the government is involved in a conspiracy to cover up these sorts of sightings, but so far it's merely conjecture and impossible to make any sort of definite conclusion. Either way, Jennifer and her husband were sure they had seen a large, unidentifiable animal in their small stretch of woods.

Area near the location of the homeless camp in San Antonio
(Photo by Lyle Blackburn)

Being that the camp was located within a reasonably populated spot near San Antonio's Sea World resort, it seems rather unlikely that a large creature such as Bigfoot could roam the area without a considerable number of sighting reports, yet stranger things have been reported over the years—things that tend to support the notion that these animals might occasionally roam areas we may not expect.

When the story of the 911 call was aired on local television stations around San Antonio, it prompted more people to come forth with older stories. One man said he grew up in the nearby county of Bandera in a tiny town nestled in the Texas Hill Country. As a kid in the 1970s, he used to play with another boy who came to visit his grandmother (who lived nearby) every summer. One afternoon when he arrived at the neighbor's house to hang out, he found the kid in distress. The kid said he had stayed up late the night before and happened to look out the window around 3:00 a.m. To his horror, he saw a "huge man-thing walk very briskly down another neighbor's long gravel driveway and disappear into the darkness and woods behind their house."[78] The neighbor had a streetlight on their carport that lit the whole area at night, so he could clearly see the thing in an unobstructed view from about seventy-five yards away. He said the thing was walking on two legs as it covered about fifty yards very quickly.

The young man wasn't sure whether to believe his friend at the time, but a few days later they were out riding dirt bikes in a nearby wooded area when his opinion changed. As they got deeper into the woods, the kid who had seen the hairy thing began to panic and cry. He was so fearful of the woods, thinking the creature might be out there, he became emphatic they leave the area. He seemed genuinely upset.

Human population in the area has continued to increase, even in the last few years, yet there is still the occasional report of a what can only be called a Bigfoot. Just one hour northeast of San

Antonio, in the Canyon Lake area of Startzville, a resident had a dramatic sighting in the winter of 2015. According to a report filed with the Bigfoot Field Researchers Organization, he and his family were in the car and backing out of their driveway at about 5:30 p.m. The weather was poor with a hazy, misty rain, and temperatures were just above freezing, so he switched on the vehicle's high-beam lights for better visibility.

"As I backed out of the driveway, my lights caught the attention of a very big creature," the witness said. "[It was] about 9 foot tall, grayish blonde in color with a 4 to 4-1/2 foot across from shoulder to shoulder."[79] The thing was standing in front of an oak tree about forty yards from the driveway. It was standing with its arms at its side and turned to look when the headlights hit it. The witness asked his son to look, turning away for a moment as he did. When he looked back, the creature was gone.

A few days later his wife and stepdaughter were walking nearby along the shore of Canyon Lake when they discovered the lifeless body of a deer. It appeared the animal's neck had been twisted and broken. The vital organs were gone, leaving only blood and a few guts. It appeared to have been partially eaten by some kind of predator.

The similarities to the incident a few years earlier at the homeless campsite—with the dead deer and sighting of a huge animal—cannot be overlooked. It could simply be coincidence, but then again, perhaps not.

Ape-X

A number of witnesses have reported seeing Bigfoot harvesting small and large animals, suggesting they are most likely omnivorous. This stands to reason since a creature of such massive size would require a high-calorie diet in order to survive. This could pose a problem if they were strictly herbivores living in pine forest habitats, where there is a lack of high-energy, plant-based food sources. The creatures would presumably harvest berries, roots, nuts, grasses, and other foraging foods, but these meals would need to be supplemented with fish, insects, and animals such as squirrels, turtles, deer, hogs, and even elk. As the ultimate apex predator, Bigfoot should have no problem in this pursuit. This may explain the discoveries of deer that are seemingly killed in a strange manner such as having their necks twisted, not to mention cases where witnesses claim to have actually seen these creatures in the act of picking up animals, as in the San Antonio incident.

In the southern United States, hogs seem to be a particular favorite when it comes to the Bigfoot diet. More than a few witnesses have reported seeing these creatures stalking wild hogs or snatching domesticated ones from outdoor pens. A shocking example of this habit occurred in 1989.

On the afternoon of July 1, Bill Simmons got an urgent call from his good friend Eddie, who lived in the rural area of Hunt County near the Sulphur River Bottoms. Eddie said that he was in the house when he heard one of his hogs continually squealing and snorting in the pen behind the home. Eddie finally grabbed his 30-30 rifle and headed outside to see what was wrong. When he looked toward the pen, he was shocked to see a huge, ape-like creature trying to lift his prize boar up and over the wooden pallet that was being used as fencing. The creature was bulky with chocolate-reddish hair covering its body, and it was definitely not scared of formidable pig.

With his hands shaking nervously, Eddie raised his rifle and fired several times at the creature. The bullets went astray, and the creature immediately dropped the hog and took off running toward the woods. Eddie was too afraid to pursue it. The boar weighed nearly five hundred pounds and was a truly dangerous animal. It had once pinned Eddie in the pen and nearly injured him. For something to even tangle with this hog was a bold act, much less lift it over the fencing.

Eddie retreated into the house and calmed his nerves. He then phoned his friend Bill Simmons and told him what had happened.

"He called me, and he was extremely shook up," Simmons told me as we discussed the event. "So myself and my dad, we hopped into my Jeep and drove over there to investigate."

Once Simmons and his father arrived, Eddie showed them an area around the pen where several sets of large, five-toed footprints had been left. These appeared to have been made by three individuals of varying sizes. The largest print was eighteen inches long, while another appeared to be around sixteen inches and the smallest at approximately twelve inches. The sixteen-inch tracks were the clearest and presumably those that belonged to the creature trying to take the hog.

"You could see the tracks up to the pallet fence," Simmons told me. "And they went off toward the woods."

The three men were not sure what to make of the situation. At the time Bigfoot was just not something they thought about or even considered, yet it appeared that whatever was trying to steal the hog fit the very profile of a Sasquatch.

This was not the first time some of Eddie's livestock had fallen prey to bizarre circumstances. Eddie and Bill had often purchased dairy bulls, which they kept on Eddie's property. A year ago, they found several of them dead with their necks twisted in a strange fashion, as if something huge had attacked them. Several of Eddie's hogs had simply disappeared with no trace. Now the men were beginning to suspect that the ape-like creature—or creatures—had been responsible.

At that point they obtained some casting material and began casting the best example of the footprint. Simmons's father was a retired Dallas police officer who had experience with investigations, so he was familiar with the process. It just so happened that Eddie's neighbor across the road had also worked for the Dallas Police Department, and he knew Simmons's father. While they were casting the track, he came over to see what was going on.

"The neighbor across the road was now a professor at what was then East Texas State University," Simmons explained. "I don't remember what department he was in, but I remember it was something not far from, you know, what we were doing, like anthropology. So he comes over and looks at the tracks. It piqued his interest enough that he called a couple of his students to come out and look at the tracks as well."

While they were talking to the professor, he mentioned that another neighbor had mentioned some strange incidents of vandalism that had occurred at his home. In one case the wooden screen doors of the home had been torn off and thrown in a cattle tank. The house hadn't been robbed; there was only the outside damage, which seemed rather pointless and odd.

Simmons, his father, Eddie, and the professor proceed to follow the tracks from the hog pen up into the woods. They headed in the direction of the neighbor's home where the vandalism had taken place.

"We followed this set of tracks across onto the property," Simmons said. "The tracks go right up by the house, and that's where we lost them. But in looking around, there were what looked like Sasquatch tracks around the house; it completely encircled it. Nothing good enough to cast, but this is what we could see."

Given the evidence, the men speculated that the vandal could have very well been a Sasquatch. Perhaps it was looking for more livestock and ripped the screens off while searching. It was all very strange and alarming to all of the homeowners.

After speaking with the neighbor, the men returned to Eddie's hog pen, where the college students finished taking photos and documenting what they could.

"We had our cast, we documented everything, so there was really nothing to do other than compare stories and scratch heads at that point." Simmons explained.

Simmons assured me that Eddie was not the kind of guy to pull a prank or play around. If he said he saw an unidentified creature, then his word was good. "I'd known him for years," Simmons assured me. "It had him shook up enough that he was stuttering and shaking his head."

Simmons didn't know what to do with the information at the time, but after seeing a television program in 2001 that featured the Texas Bigfoot Research Center, he reached out to the group. The TBRC responded and was able to facilitate an examination of the footprint cast by Jimmy Chilcutt, a retired police officer who had worked as a fingerprint examiner for the Conroe Police Department in Texas. Chilcutt has evaluated several suspected Sasquatch tracks and in some cases found what he believes to be "dermal ridges" (like fingerprints) that are neither human nor known primate. According to Chilcutt, they appear to be a "species in itself."[80] After examining the track from Simmons, he concluded that it could have been left by a creature that we have yet to document. A creature that appears to be roaming the woods and dining on the very same livestock and wild game as many of its fellow Texans!

The track casting made in Hunt County on July 1, 1989
(Photo by Bill Simmons)

Detail of the Hunt County track. Note the possible dermal ridges.
(Photo by Bill Simmons)

5.

WILDER WEST

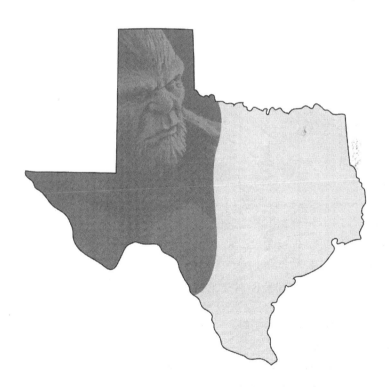

When it comes to traditional Bigfoot habitat, or at least what we imagine it to be, the western portion of Texas doesn't seem to match at all. In the flat, dusty expanse of the Panhandle's High Plains to the Southwestern Tablelands of the Trans-Pecos near El Paso, one would expect to see a wayward gunslinger far more than a mysterious ape. Yet here again, we find a handful of classic and compelling stories that have often been publicized in newspapers or investigated by credible researchers.

These cases may seem out of place in terms of the usual Bigfoot reports, but this is Texas. The sparsely populated scrublands that make up a good portion of the state may be ideal for creatures that want to enjoy some solitude as long as they don't mind a bit of hot weather. Or perhaps they are only passing through. There have been a number of Bigfoot sightings in the neighboring state of New Mexico, and some of those sighting locations are close to the border of West Texas. Either way, these intriguing cases add yet another layer of wild mystery to the ever-growing story.

Caddo Critter

"It looked like a gorilla!" Charlie Gantt said in a stern voice as he told a reporter from the *Abilene Reporter-News* about a strange incident that happened just days before. It was July 21, 1964, and Gantt, along with fellow resident John Mitchell, were being interviewed about a mysterious creature they had both claimed to see near the small town of Caddo in Stephens County.[81]

Gantt said that on Saturday, July 18, he was at his country home when he saw a huge animal with dark fur creeping from the woods. It was so alarming he grabbed his long-barreled,.22 caliber pistol and fired at it, apparently missing it since the creature, which he said stood upward of seven feet tall and measured at least four feet in width, retreated into the woods.

As wild as the incident sounded, Gantt was not the only resident to have seen the thing. John Mitchell, who was also being interview by the newspaper, said he first saw the beast three weeks earlier. Since then, he'd seen it three times. Once it emerged from a mesquite brush near his trailer home and attacked his dog. Mitchell was not sure the reporter believed him. "Looks like we're gonna have to kill it and put it under their noses to convince them!" he quipped to Gantt during the interview.

Stories of a large, rather undefined type creature had long existed in the tiny town's lore. Residents referred to it as the "Caddo Critter," sometimes using it as the butt of a joke, and sometimes insisting they had seen it. At the time, Caddo boasted a mere fifty citizens, so pretty much everyone was familiar with the resident Critter. Gantt was one of them, except this time he was shocked when it visited his property. His friends and neighbors remarked that he was not one to tell lies, so whatever he claimed to see, many took him at his word.

Mitchell and Gantt were not the only ones who had a recent encounter with the Caddo Critter. Gene Couch, a nine-year-old boy who lived close to Mitchell, said he came upon it while he was walking to a fishing hole on Saturday afternoon. He was so frightened he fled back home and told his mother. Mrs. Couch told the reporter: "I don't know what Gene saw, but he came running back white as a sheet." She added that something had also been fighting with their dogs.

John Mitchell's wife, who was a neighbor, heard Gene's story and hurried to the spot where the boy said he'd seen it. Sure enough the thing was still lingering in the vicinity, and Mrs. Mitchell got a good look as the thing growled and started throwing rocks in her direction. All the witnesses concurred it "looked like a gorilla." This was curious, because there was seemingly no way a gorilla would be loose in the area.

Sheriff Edgar Martin echoed the sentiment, saying: "There

just aren't any gorillas in this country."[82] He surmised that it was either a person who was being mistaken for an ape or perhaps a male deer. The witnesses scoffed, remaining steadfast in their assessment of a very big, ape-like animal.

Such doubts did not discourage people from attempting to hunt the Critter. Several of the locals grabbed their firearms and began searching the thinly wooded areas surrounding Caddo. The searches yielded no results, however.

When news of the creature sightings hit the papers, folks in the area began to wonder if the Caddo Critter was perhaps the same strange animal seen the year before near the town of Haskell sixty miles east. In the summer of 1963, residents of that area had reported sightings of a large, "shaggy" creature that was suspected of killing livestock on some of the local ranches. The thing was dubbed "The Varmint" or the "Haskell Rascal" by local reporters who surmised it might be a massive mountain lion despite the fact that no mountain lions (i.e., cougars) were thought to live in the area.[83] Either way, the creature was described as being a quadruped with light-colored fur and a height of approximately four feet at the shoulder. This did not match the tall, dark, ape-like profile of the Caddo Critter, so it's unlikely they were the same beast.

Back in Caddo, the local residents kept a wary eye on the woods, but all was quiet until August 1 when two young men from the city of Arlington claimed they captured footage of the elusive beast on film. According to an article in the *Fort Worth Star-Telegram*, the film was shot in the woods south of Caddo by LeRoy Yarbrough (22) and Jerry Oakes (23). Yarbrough claimed he had hunted the Caddo Critter off and on since 1955 and on that night came within twenty yards of it. The "movie film" was aired on WBAP-TV. It showed "a hairy black figure resembling a gorilla walking on two legs."[84] The film is rather blurry and undefined, so reporters admitted it could have been a person dressed in a costume.

Such was the truth. A few days later it came to light that Yarbrough had been pranked by his friends. When Yarbrough announced he was going on a hunt for the Caddo Critter, one of his friends followed along, dressed up in a costume, and fooled him into thinking he had actually encountered the beast.[85]

By now, Caddo citizens were growing tired of the news circus and felt embarrassed by the whole affair. Most of them did not believe in the Critter, although no one had been able to explain just what the witnesses had seen. A rancher named Harold Cook suggested it could have been his yak. The animal, which was dark brown in color and had small horns, had wandered away from his ranch months earlier.[86] It was as good of an explanation as any, so residents were happy to let the story die as no more sightings of the odd beast were reported.

Interestingly enough, a hunter from Breckenridge claimed to have encountered a Bigfoot near Caddo in 1994. The hunter, identified as Jeff, told an interviewer at Dixie Cryptid he was sitting in a deer blind early one morning when he felt something press against it. When he looked out the window opening, he was shocked to see a tall, ape-like animal with gray hair literally scratching its back on the structure. The creature turned and looked right into the eyes of the hunter. Jeff said it was so startling, he accidentally pulled the trigger of a pistol he was holding, shooting a hole in the bottom of the blind. When the gun went off, the creature screamed and took off running at an incredible speed. Jeff described it as being approximately eight feet tall and "looking human in the face."[87] The hunter said he'd heard tales of the Caddo Critter all of his life, but to be confronted with such an experience was something he could have never imagined.

Caddo Critter news article from July 22, 1964
(Abilene Reporter-News)

Hawley Him

Eighty miles west of Caddo and forty miles south of Haskell lies the small, dusty town of Hawley where another creature scare rocked the locals in 1977. It started on the morning of July 6, 1977, as Tom Roberts (14) and Larry Suggs (15) were working at the Abilene Boys' Ranch owned by Mr. Bob Scott. The boys had been clearing brush for Mr. Scott that morning and were taking a break at around 10:00 a.m. when they were startled by the sound of snapping tree limbs. Seconds later, rocks began flying in their direction.

Suggs was hit in the leg by one of the rocks while others just barely missed their heads. The boys threw down their tools and ran for the safety of a nearby home owned by Ed McFarland. Before fleeing, however, they managed to get "three good glimpses" of their assailant. "It was kind of an ape, but still a man," Suggs told newspaper reporters. "He had huge arms. They hung to his knees."[88] Roberts said the thing didn't make any vocalizations or other noises. They only heard the sound of breaking branches. He also said they noticed a terrible "rotten smell" just prior to the attack.

When the boys arrived at the McFarland home they found their friend, Renee McFarland (15), and told her what they had seen. Renee suggested they grab one of her father's rifles and head back to confront the ape-man. (The newspaper articles are not clear as to whether Renee's father was also home at the time.)

When the trio returned to the site of the attack, they spotted the creature lingering about forty yards away. Renee handed the gun to Larry Suggs, who volunteered to take a shot. Suggs raised the rifle to his shoulder, aimed as best he could, and fired. The shot missed the ape-thing as the gun's recoil sent Suggs tumbling backward. The loud noise was enough, however, to send the creature running into the brush. "That stuff (the brush) is so thick you have to know where you're going and he just glided through it," Roberts explained.

Authorities were doubtful that a "monster" was loose in the area, but "long footprints" were found in the sandy soil where the youths said it had been standing. In addition, the man who owned the ranch said he'd recently lost twenty-one goats from a pen. They had disappeared without a trace, save for a couple of carcasses found in the brush a few days later. The Jones County Sheriff concluded that coyotes were to blame, but the rancher argued that it was unlikely since not a single goat was killed inside the pen.

This incident was not the first sighting of the creature. Renee McFarland told reporters she had seen it the previous October, but when she told her parents they dismissed her story as fantasy. Another resident, Mike McQuagge, claimed to have seen the same long footprints, although he had never seen the beast itself.

When news of the incident made headlines, reporters were quick to give the ape-man a monstrous moniker. Because Suggs had referred to it as a "him," it was officially dubbed the Hawley Him.

The resulting news piqued the interest of would-be monster hunters who began to descend on Bob Scott's ranch. The first group consisted of three students from Abilene College who hoped "to study the creature's habitat."[89] Scott granted them permission to look around on a Friday night.

The second group of Hawley Him hunters consisted of Ed Nash and his stepson, David Woods. Nash claimed to have had an encounter with a similar ape-like thing in the backwoods of West Virginia in 1964. With the appearance of the Hawley Him, he felt compelled to prove its existence to the world. "I would turn it (the creature) over to science so we can find out what the heck it is," Nash told reporters at the time.[90]

Bob Scott granted Nash and Woods access to his ranch. On the Sunday following the initial search by the college students (which yielded no evidence), Nash and Woods entered the ranch property armed with a .30 caliber carbine rifle. They were accompanied by a news reporter who brought along a loaded 35 mm camera.

The duo proceeded to comb the groves of stunted oak trees and tangled brush looking for any signs of the creature. The ground cover was quite thick, so they mainly stuck to game trails that crisscrossed the property. The men found evidence that "big game" had used the trail, but it was hard to find any tracks that may have belonged to the Hawley Him. It had not only rained on Friday and Saturday nights, washing out the soil, but there were numerous boot prints stamped upon most of the game trails. It appeared that the monster hunters who had visited before them left more signs than the Hawley Him itself.

Nash and Woods did eventually find a long, abandoned dirt road deep in the shinnery (a dense growth of scrub oak trees), where they discovered a fresh footprint that appeared to have been made by the creature. It showed the impression of four toes and the ball of a foot with a stride of four feet. Nash concluded there must be something unusual out there, but they could not locate it at present. The men decided to return again later after the monster fever had died down so they could more effectively search for footprints and, ultimately, the titular creature itself.

In mid-August, after no new sightings of the Hawley Him had been reported, a West Texas oilman named Jack Grimm came forward to offer a considerable reward. He promised $5,000 for the "safe capture of the evasive creature." The rules specified that the creature be previously unidentified and undiscovered, and not merely an escaped zoo primate.[91]

Grimm was a trained geologist who ran his own drilling operations. He was skeptical that a large, ape-like creature would be roaming the scrublands of the Abilene area but was deeply interested in the potential discovery of any cryptids. Over the years he had subsidized searches for Bigfoot in the Pacific Northwest and the Loch Ness Monster in Scotland. One of the film crews he sent to Loch Ness actually "photographed a fuzzy outline of what the oilman thinks is the Loch Ness creature." He felt it would be a significant contribution to science if one of these creatures were discovered, and that included the Bigfoot-like creature on his own turf of Texas. As things go in these pursuits, however, no one was ever able to cash in on the reward. The Hawley Him fervor quietly died down and the creature, if there was one, seemingly moved on.

Jones County returned to normal daily life, but it wasn't without at least one more strange report years later. On September 17, 2001, a photographer was driving in the area of Lake Fork Phantom Hill just a few miles east of Hawley at around 1:00 a.m. when he spotted something unusual in the road.

"I was driving down the lake bridge to go to take shots of a thunderstorm," the photographer explained. "I was on the bridge heading east and my lights caught something large about 50 yards from the exit."[92]

The man stopped and observed the figure. "The thing sat there for a while and just looked at me," he continued. "From what I gathered, it was about 7–8 foot tall, well over 500 pounds. The fur was not black, more of a brown, but then again it was dark."

The photographer got the impression the creature was trying to protect something so he thought it would be best to back his car off the bridge rather than try to pass the animal. The car window was down, and before he left, the witness could hear the creature making some kind of grunting or "crackling" sound. It was followed by a similar sound that came from the nearby woods. Something was presumably answering the creature on the bridge.

It was a dark night as the thunderstorm brewed over the lake and the surrounding woods of Phantom Hill—not the place to confront strange creatures. The driver hurriedly backed up his car and sped out of the area, leaving us with one pertinent question. If he was a photographer with a camera, why didn't he take a photo? It is yet another mystery within this Texas-sized enigma.

Youths Report Attack
By the 'Hawley Him'

By ROGER DOWNING
Staff Writer

HAWLEY — The forest of the Northwest has its Big Foot, the Himalayas have the Abominable Snowman and, as of Wednesday, this dusty Jones County town has the Hawley Him.

The Him, a shaggy 7-foot monster with long dangling arms, reportedly attacked three youths Wednesday morning at Bob Scott's ranch.

The youths, Tom Roberts, 14; Larry Suggs, 15; and Renee McFarland, 13, all reported seeing the beast and even tried to down the critter with a shot from a 30-30 rifle before the apparition made good his escape in the thick brush.

The reported attack started at approximately 10 a.m. while Roberts and Suggs were clearing brush for Scott. Both the boys live at the Abilene Boys' Ranch, of which Scott is superintendent. The boys said they were taking a break when they were startled by the breaking of tree limbs and a shower of rocks.

Suggs said he was hit in the leg by one of the stony missiles and showed a

See HIM'S A
Back page this section

A FOOT-LONG FOOTPRINT
...left in the sandy soil of Jones County?

'Hawley Him' targets

These three youths say they were the targets Wednesday of the Hawley Him. From left are Tom Roberts, Renee McFarland and Larry Suggs. (Staff Photo by Mark Allred)

Hawley Him news article from July 7, 1977

(Abilene Reporter-News)

Panhandlers

Far to the north, in the "panhandle" region of Texas, there's a much different landscape. Here, we find vast areas of flat, open plains and shrub savanna flanked by red-hued canyons, mesas, and swaths of badlands. It's a vista that would provide an impressive backdrop for any epic western movie. By day, it's bathed in bright heat as the sun warms the buffalo grass of the rangelands, while by night, the dry winds howl with eerie echoes through lonely canyons. One would fully expect to see a pack of wild coyotes or a weathered cowboy saunter by at any moment—a Bigfoot, however, not so much. Yet the arid badlands do have their mysteries to offer.

One such case dates back to 1975. That year, eighteen-year-old Paul Mackey was living in Chicago where he and his best friend worked at a local steak restaurant. One night while working, they decided on a whim they should head to California where the sun was more appealing than the perpetually cold winters. The young men subsequently packed up a '63 Volkswagen and struck out along Route 66 for the West Coast.

The promise of adventure may have been high, but the reliability of the old VW was low. As they were driving through Oklahoma, a warning light on the dash began to flicker on and off. Paul insisted they stop and check the oil, but his friend (who owned the car) pressed on until they eventually crossed the state line into Texas. It was there that disaster finally struck. About fifty miles shy of Amarillo, the car seized up and sputtered to the side of the road.

The two young men sat there for a moment taking in the scenery. It was dark and very cold, and mostly deserted with only an occasional passing vehicle. It seemed to be the worst place for a breakdown. Fortunately, a trucker eventually stopped and offered assistance. Paul's friend asked the trucker if he could drive him somewhere to buy some oil so he could get the VW started again.

Paul decided to stay behind with their car and belongings. He watched as the truck carrying his friend disappeared into the distance. An impressive, starlit sky hung overhead, but its beauty did little to stave off the unnerving feeling of being left alone in such a remote place.

Paul got in the back seat and tried to sleep, but he couldn't. He stared out the window, watching as tumbleweeds blew across the highway and rolled off into the darkness that surrounded the car. In a letter to Craig Woolheater of the Texas Bigfoot Research Center, Paul explained the harrowing incident that occurred next:

I remember a freight train off to the North crossing the prairie and I remember thinking how desolate it looked outside. It was now around 1:30 a.m. and I happened to look across the highway to my left watching another tumbleweed blow across the road; then I saw it, a huge, furry looking figure walking upright toward the road. I was speechless and crouched down in the back seat and tried to cover myself under a blanket. This creature was at least eight feet tall. It stopped on the shoulder in front of the car and stooped down as a human would and looked into the car through the windshield. In the dim light, I could see it was furry and massive in girth around its shoulders. Its face was shadowy and I could not see its eyes. I let out a blood-curdling scream and kept screaming. The creature stood up and continued walking out into the prairie until I could not see it anymore. I pinched myself to be sure I was awake. I had not been sleeping [and it] was not my imagination!

A truck eventually stopped across the road and Paul's friend got out. Paul had never been so relieved to see someone in his life. He hurriedly told his friend about the strange sighting, but as these things often go, his friend merely laughed. Despite

Paul's insistence that he was not dreaming and that it was not a bear, he was unable to convince his friend that whatever he had seen was not a normal animal.

"I have kept this to myself because when I have told the story I was met with incredulous looks and remarks," he said. What his friend and others may not realize is that Paul is not the only person to have seen something unexplainable walking the lonely roads of the Texas plains.

In November 2001, three motorcyclists were riding through Baily County in the Panhandle when two of them nearly collided with a humanoid creature. It was a cool night with a patchy, light fog that hung above their heads as they rode in single-file fashion through the open ranch lands near Muleshoe National Wildlife Refuge. The first rider, who was in the lead by about one quarter mile, did not see anything. The second rider, however, noticed a tall, light-colored animal crossing a ditch and heading into the road. It wouldn't be uncommon for an animal to dart across the desolate road, except this thing was upright on two legs. The rider instinctively swerved as he believed the thing was about to cross his path. The third rider, who was close behind, saw his friend swerve. When he reached the thing, it was now standing completely in the road, towering above his bike. He had to swerve drastically to avoid hitting it. The thing then continued across the road and vanished into the darkness beyond.

Shaken by the incident, the men immediately pulled over and began comparing their recollections. They had both seen the very same thing. "It was about seven feet tall and white," the second rider reported to the Texas Bigfoot Research Conservancy. "It was standing upright and seemed to have red eyes [and] it had long arms."[93] They both agreed it looked humanesque but was definitely not a human.

The men kept the story mostly to themselves until one of them came across an article about Bigfoot in the October 2005 issue of *Texas Highways* magazine. It was then that he submitted the details to the TBRC. Investigator Daryl Colyer followed up by interviewing all three men. He noted that the third man, who had gotten the best look at the thing, was certain it was at least six feet in height or perhaps taller, as it seemed to tower over him as he passed. He and his friends had no suitable explanation for what they encountered that night. All they knew was that it was large, upright, and covered in hair, and even though it moved on two legs and behaved as a human, it was simply not human.

A lonely road outside of Amarillo

(Photo by Lyle Blackburn)

Bugs and the Bigfoot Murders

On June 5, 2001, a man who identified himself only as "Bugs" and Bigfoot researcher, Robert W. Morgan, were guests on the popular syndicated radio show, *Coast To Coast AM*, hosted by Art Bell. The show (which still airs today with host, George Noory) features a variety of guests who discuss topics such as cryptids, ghosts, conspiracies, UFOs, and other strange phenomena. On this particular episode, Bugs had been asked to recount a rather disturbing story in which he claims to have killed two Bigfoots while hunting near his home in the Texas Panhandle.[94] Bugs, who had told the story on the show previously, said he "trusted" Bell, and would therefore be willing share more details even though he feared authorities might prosecute him for killing the creatures. To protect himself, he used the alias "Bugs" for all of his radio appearances.

According to Bugs, in February 1976 he and two friends were hunting bobcats one night when they spotlighted a huge, hairy animal standing on two legs. The men were so startled, they fired at it with their high-powered rifles. The creature fell down but managed to get back up and flee. It ran toward a creek at the edge of a field and disappeared into the darkness.

Bugs said he and his buddies followed the blood trail to a plum thicket where they could hear something growling within. Bugs was carrying a.44 Magnum handgun, so he was nominated to crawl into thicket to see what they had shot. At that point the men weren't sure if it was a bear or something else.

The brush of the thicket was so dense, Bugs said he had to literally crawl on his hands and knees to enter it. Once inside, he was confronted by a female Bigfoot who was presumably protecting the injured one. Bugs said he shot her in the chest at point-blank range. The massive creature fell over, but just as the other creature had, it sprang up and advanced toward him. Bugs fired two more shots, which finally killed it.

After the melee, Bugs could see a male creature lying dead just beyond the body of the female. It was obvious they were mates. Bugs said the creatures were very human-like despite their large, apish bodies. Yet they had six toes on each foot, which is an odd trait for primate or human. Robert Morgan, who was one of the first men to embark on a serious investigation of the Sasquatch phenomenon in the late 1960s, interjected saying there was evidence of a Bigfoot family living in the Ozarks region of Arkansas who appeared to have six toes. Either way, Bugs insisted the creatures were real and that he and his friends had shot them. He even claimed to have taken a dozen Polaroid photos of their dead bodies. Bugs said that after the shooting, he and his friends pulled the bodies from the plum thicket and buried them along Elm Creek, a tributary of the Red River.

During the conversation, Bugs seemed truly remorseful of his actions and expressed fear that he would face legal charges if he were to be identified. Bugs claimed he was so traumatized by the event he no longer hunted or would ever return to the burial site. The site had been kept a closely guarded secret, but Bugs trusted Art Bell enough to provide him with a confidential map showing the alleged location where the Bigfoots had been buried. Bell, not knowing what to do with it, eventually convinced Bugs to give it to Robert Morgan, believing he could help.

Because *Coast To Coast* is such a widely syndicated show, the story became a hot topic among Bigfoot enthusiasts, especially those living in Texas. Once again, the Panhandle seemed like an unlikely spot for a Bigfoot family to be living, but the sincerity with which Bugs confessed to the shooting gave it an air of credibility.

Not surprisingly, many armchair sleuths attempted to uncover Bugs's true identity. They also sought a copy of the map, which not been made public. Based on the location of "Elm Creek," it could only be determined that the incident happened somewhere near Shamrock, Texas, east of Amarillo.

For years, the tragic story of the Texas Bigfoot Murders was debated online and around campfires until the truth of the matter finally came out in 2009 when some astute writers at the now defunct blog known as The Regular realized Bugs sounded very much like the controversial radio personality, Ed Hale. Hale, who lived in the Texas town of Wellington, was the producer of *Plains Radio*, a show that was known for radical viewpoints. Once outed, Hale somewhat "confessed" on his radio show, admitting that he is indeed Bugs, but held steadfast that the story of the dead Bigfoots was true. However, don't expect to find the bodies. Hale said "federal agents" had long since shown up at his house and forced him to dig up the remains which were by then nothing but bones. The feds allegedly confiscated everything, leaving Hale with no way to prove his story.[95]

Terrain of the Texas Panhandle

(Photo by Lyle Blackburn)

This, for better or worse, seems to be a typical excuse for the lack of physical evidence in cases where Bigfoot bodies are concerned. The federal agent scenario is one that has been offered in several other cases where people have claimed to have shot one of these creatures yet could not produce any supporting evidence.

The Bugs story still reverberates as a low note in Texas Bigfoot history, but in the end it is perhaps a relief that no Bigfoots were actually harmed . . . unless, of course, the rhetoric of an extremely shady character and the conspiracy theories therein are actually true.

Horizon City Monster

At the far western end of Texas, nestled into the crux of the jutting boundary tip where the Lone Star State meets Old Mexico and New Mexico, lies the notorious town of El Paso. The now sprawling city, often heralded by song and film, boasts a mix of Texan and Mexican heritage that melds together in unique blend of arid atmosphere and colorful culture. It is a place where, on its outskirts, one might expect to see a soaring Thunderbird of ancient myth or a toothy Blue Dog (a.k.a. Chupacabra) running amok, but not a Bigfoot. However, as we've come to expect from this exploration into hairy Texas history, there is always a surprise.

In September 1975, in the community of Horizon City just east of El Paso, two teenagers were hanging out near a golf course one evening when they saw a primal, hairy figure walking on two legs across the green. According to an article in the *El Paso Times*, Billy Fuller (14) and Kathy Ellis (15) were minding their own business when they looked up to see the strange sight.

"It ducked down to the ground and just took off," Miss Ellis told a reporter who interviewed the teens.[96]

As luck would have it, an officer from the sheriff's department drove by moments after the incident. Fuller and Ellis frantically flagged down the vehicle and told the officer, Bill Rutherford, what they had seen. Rutherford shined his light in the direction where the entity had been walking, but he did not see anything.

"We know we saw it, but Mr. Rutherford says he never did. I think he said that just so people would not start getting scared," Ellis said.

Ellis also told reporters that she and Fuller were not the first to have seen it. She had recently heard about a woman who allegedly had a close encounter. "There was a lady who nearly hit it with her car," she explained. "But I don't know who she was."

As the weeks progressed, other teenagers claimed to have seen the strange creature lurking about. Bill York (15) was among them. He said he got a good look at the creature on the golf course driving range. "His face was all pushed in and flat like a bulldog's. And he had this big nose that stuck out," York said. "His eyes were sunk in deep and his jaw jutted out."

More details were provided by other eyewitnesses. The thing was generally reported as being about "8 feet tall, 3-1/2 feet wide and leaving footprints 14 inches long 8 inches wide." It was covered in hair and had "pointed ears."

One boy reportedly got close enough to shoot at the creature with a rifle. He was apparently dove hunting near the golf course at the time, so he had a firearm. He said he hit it at least six times at close range with bird shot. However, no blood was ever found. The whole thing sounded bizarre, but the teens were adamant they were not making up the stories.

As for the tracks, some of them were apparently destroyed by vehicles and some by would-be monster hunters who were now tromping around the vicinity looking for the thing. Deputy Rutherford said he personally saw two of the tracks in the soft desert sand. They led away from the golf course and were about twenty feet apart. They were the only ones he saw, and in his opinion, they had been "dug."

The newspaper referred to the creature as the "Horizon City Monster" as it relayed the details. The resulting coverage fueled a fire of speculation and eventually attracted outside attention. Deputy Rutherford told reporters that among the amateur monster hunters there were two anthropologists from the University of Southern California who had traveled across the country to have a look for themselves. As these things tend to go, they returned to the west coast empty-handed.

"I know a lot of the people around here don't believe we saw anything," young Kathy Ellis said. "But there really was something out there. And it really scared us bad."

When the creature failed to make a return appearance after September, the hubbub eventually faded out like the sporadic desert winds. But the Horizon City Monster was not forgotten. In 2003, a man who had been living in Horizon City during the 1975 incidents made a report to the Texas Bigfoot Research Center detailing how he had actually seen some strange footprints himself. The man said he was out by the golf course with a friend on the night of September 12, 1975, when they discovered large, five-toed footprints tromping through some creosote bushes[ix] and onto a sand dune. They returned the next day and followed the trackway as it progressed across the sand for nearly a quarter mile. The tracks stopped where the granules transitioned to the harder surface of the arroyo.

"The remarkable thing about the prints were [sic] that all five toes were not evident in all the prints . . . indicating the creature that made the prints had flexible toes (not like a fake foot) where the little toe and the one next to it had lifted occasionally when the prints were made," the man wrote. " Another remarkable thing about the prints were [sic] that they led often through the

---

ix A creosote bush (*Larrea tridentata*) is another name for a flowering, evergreen shrub that grows in desert environments.

middle of four-foot creosote bushes, crushing the main branches, indicating to me that the prints were not faked because a human would never have done this and risked physical injury."[97]

The tracks measured approximately seventeen inches long and seven inches wide. They were strange enough that his friend took photographs of them. According to the witness, his friend had possession of the photos, so he did not have them to submit when he made the report in 2003.

The same year (2003), a news article appeared in the *El Paso Times* heralding the possible return of the Horizon City Monster. In the article, resident Cecelia Montañez claimed she had seen a "big gorilla-like thing" near the desert three years earlier and again in October 2002. Montañez, a retired secretary, moved from El Paso to Horizon City in 2000 just before she had the first encounter.[98] The news article is scant on details, but fortunately she spoke to Craig Woolheater of the TBRC shortly thereafter and provided him with far more detail. In the conversation, Montañez explained that she was driving along the rather deserted Eastlake Boulevard at around noon on August 4, 2000, when she noticed a large, humanoid figure standing near the road up ahead. It was leaning over an object that was laying on the ground. As soon as she saw the thing, it stood up and began walking, fully upright on two legs, toward the desert to the west, perpendicular to the road. It walked in casual manner, swinging its arms naturally as it progressed up and over a sand mound. At that point it walked a bit further and then seemingly "disappeared." Montañez said she got the impression that it "went down into a cave into the desert" even though she returned the following day with her husband to investigate and could not find any such cave entrance.

Montañez described the creature as being about seven to eight feet tall, over three hundred pounds, and covered in faded, maroon hair that was uniformly short in length. It had wide shoulders, slim hips, and a muscular build that looked more ape-like than human. She could only see its facial profile, so she did not get a good look at the eyes or expression, but she could tell that it had a bulldog-shaped mouth and small, pointy ears.

Mrs. Montañez estimated that she observed the creature for approximately thirty seconds as she slowly drove toward the point in the road where she had first seen it hunched over the object. She was afraid to get out of the car but could tell the object was a dead coyote. The coyote was laying on its left side with a fresh, hand-sized blood smear on its fur. Its head had been removed with what appeared to be a clean cut, as if by a knife or other instrument. It was laying approximately fifteen feet away from the road. Montañez did not see any pools of blood on or around the carcass or head.

The witness said she was spooked, so she quickly drove from the area. The next day she returned with her husband and another man to have a look around. The coyote parts were now gone. They attempted to locate footprints in the sand but likewise found nothing, nor did they find a cave in the location where the thing had "disappeared."

Following the incident, Mrs. Montañez scoured the internet to find out if anyone else had seen such a thing in Horizon City. Sure enough, she found the news article from 1975 and the Texas Bigfoot Research Center website, where she ultimately filed a report.

Montañez claimed to have had another run-in with a mysterious ape-man in October 2002. This time she was driving home at around 9:00 p.m. when she saw an upright animal lurking in front of her neighbor's house. Its eyes glowed red as her headlights hit it. The creature briefly walked on two legs in front of the house before dropping to all fours and running swiftly down the street toward the desert. There were houses in the area, but there was plenty of open space beyond them.

The details of how the thing disappeared so quickly in

broad daylight, its pointy ears, and even the fact that it was seen in such an open desert environment are bizarre, but Montañez was presumably not the only one to have encounters. She told Woolheater that she eventually located other stories that seemed to corroborate hers.

It has been theorized that Bigfoots might utilize caves as a place of shelter and concealment, but the possibility of caves around the El Paso area is slim. Caves, such as Carlsbad Caverns in New Mexico, require limestone rock. The terrain around El Paso is mainly arid desert.

Tony Aguilar, who was the Horizon City Police Chief back in the early 2000s, had another theory. He said he'd heard about a hermit with long hair and a beard who may have lived in the mountains near Horizon City in the early 1970s. Apparently some hunters found a cave where he had been living. Perhaps the hairy man could have been the source of the sightings.

Caves, hermits, or otherwise, sightings of Horizon City's titular beast have continued. In 2019, Alfredo Hernandez was driving on the outskirts of town at 8:00 a.m. when he spotted something odd walking along the dusty roads. "As I drove through a crossroad, I saw something to my right. I turned and it was half-way across the road, but I got a good look," he told me. "It was dark, black, lean, and about seven or eight feet tall."

The thing never looked at Hernandez as he drove by; it simply kept walking away from the road into the arid landscape. Hernandez noted that the spot where he saw the unidentified figure was approximately two hundred yards from a water reservoir. Perhaps the thing had been there for a drink. If something like Bigfoot does exist in the arid flatlands of far western Texas, then water would surely be its most crucial asset.

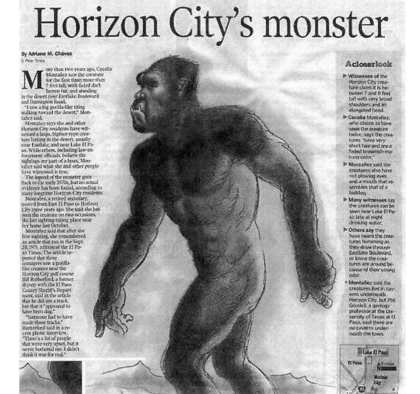

Horizon City Monster news article from July 31, 2003

(El Paso Times)

6.

THE BIGFOOT CAPITAL

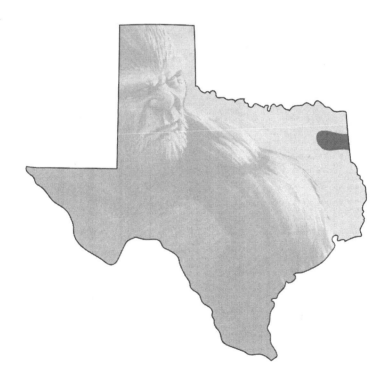

As the Texas landscape transitions eastward, from arid desert to hill country to plateaus and prairies, it eventually morphs into an area known as the Piney Woods. The lush greenery here seems like a complete world away from the open tablelands of the west, giving one the impression that it must surely be a different state altogether. But this is Texas, huge and immensely diverse.

The Piney Woods derives its name from a massive canopy of coniferous forestry dominated by several species of pine as well as hardwoods including hickory and oak. The region covers 54,400 square miles in total, spanning across eastern Texas, northwestern Louisiana, southwestern Arkansas, and southeastern Oklahoma. It is an area with a high amount of annual precipitation and rich flora that not only paints the eastern third of Texas with a wide green brush, but seems to be a perfect environment for Bigfoot, if there ever was one.

Nestled within the stately timbers of the Piney Woods and adjacent to the primitive wilds of the swampy Caddo Lake sits the small town of Jefferson in Marion County. Jefferson has long been a centerpiece of the Texas Bigfoot story as the site of an annual Texas Bigfoot Conference, an event that's been running in one form or another for more than twenty years. In recent years, Jefferson has become officially recognized by town proclamation as the "Bigfoot Capital of Texas." This accolade is not only due to the conference and the long history of Bigfoot sightings surrounding the town, but due to the efforts of Craig Woolheater, who not only organizes the annual conference, but was the founder of the Texas Bigfoot Research Center in 1999. Through this organization, its offshoots, and the associated events, the history of the Texas Bigfoot phenomenon has been documented, shared, and celebrated in a way that has ingrained the legendary creature into the very culture of East Texas. When the conference first debuted in 2000, there was little interest or knowledge of Bigfoot sightings in Texas. Now, it's much different. The conference sells out each year with a capacity crowd, consisting of both longtime enthusiasts and those with fresh curiosity. When visiting the town of Jefferson any time of year, one can find evidence of Bigfoot's popular presence by way of a huge statue of the creature, various metal cutouts of Bigfoot standing in front of stores and homes, as well as a myriad of Sasquatch-related products on sale in places such as the Jefferson General Store. Local newspapers are eager to cover the conference and any related stories, as numerous visitors drop by each year to experience the town or tromp through the Piney Woods in search of the mysterious beast itself.

The enthusiasm for Bigfoot is not confined to Jefferson or even the Piney Woods, of course, as it's become an increasingly beloved subject across North America. Yet the transformation of Jefferson into the Bigfoot Capital of Texas surely represents vibrant proof of the subject's popularity in the Lone Star State as a whole.

That being said, Jefferson is not just tourist culture and conferences. It is indeed a hub of Bigfoot activity that spans back more than sixty years when dramatic accounts of sightings and monster hunts first made headlines in its small-town newspaper. It is a story that resonates across the Piney Woods like the very howl of the creature itself.

Marion County Monster

On August 20, 1965, thirteen-year-old Johnny Maples was walking on a rural road in Marion County near Jefferson when he heard a noise in the bushes. He thought it might be a friend who lived nearby, so he called out. When no one answered, he threw a few rocks into the bushes, figuring it was just a small animal. Suddenly, a "large hairy man or beast" emerged from the trees behind a fence, presumably having been hit by one of the rocks. It jumped over the fence and started toward him. Maples panicked and started running.

"I ran as hard and fast as I could, but he kept up with me and he wasn't running, either, just sort of walking along behind me," Maples told a reporter from the *Marshall News Messenger*.[99] The boy kept running, all the while looking back to see the hairy beast in pursuit. "The last time I turned around the beast had gone off the road and disappeared into the woods," he explained. "I could hear him moving around but I didn't see him again."

A neighbor eventually drove by and gave Johnny a ride home. When the boy told the story to his mother (who noted her son was in a "state of shock"), she immediately called the Marion County Sheriff's Office. A deputy was sent to the scene, but he could find no evidence of the alleged beast. Maples described it as a seven-foot-tall ape with long, black hair all over its body except for the face, stomach, and palms of its hands, which, he noted, "hung down below his knees."

Shortly after the Maples incident, Mary Manning and her daughter Rosemary were at the Old Foundry Cemetery on the north side of Jefferson when they heard a loud, guttural growl come from the woods. It sounded like a big animal. The next day, Mrs. Manning and her husband, Herbert, returned to the cemetery to have a look around. At the back of the lot, outside the fence, they found a set of "huge tracks" that led to a small creek in the woods. Thinking they could lure in the animal, they left a pile of green pears beside the path.[100] (Brave folks!)

Four days later, the pears were gone, and fresh tracks were visible in the dirt. Several men came out to inspect the tracks, including Keith Thompson of Marshall, who cast them in plaster. The tracks were not extremely large but were curious enough to preserve. Marion County Deputy Sheriff Bill Freese said he first believed they were left by a bear (small black bears have been known to inhabit the woods surrounding Jefferson). He changed his mind, however, once he viewed the tracks. They didn't appear to be that of a bear, though he did not know what had made them. Some theorized the tracks were made by the same creature that chased Maples, which the newspaper dubbed the "Marion County Monster."

While the investigators and hunters were inspecting the tracks, Bubba Turner, a man who lived near the cemetery, came down and told them his cattle had been "all in bunch" the day before. He said they do that when scared. Turner said he decided to look around and eventually walked down a path that led to the creek. There he spotted "two large, black figures of some sort." He was too afraid to approach them, so he ran back to his house and "watched through a window until the objects disappeared down the trail."[101]

As the newspapers relayed the various stories, carloads of curiosity seekers came to investigate while others came forth telling of their own strange experiences in the area. One of these people was Richard Eason, who had worked as a conductor for the Texas and Pacific (T&P) Railroad years before. Eason told the *Longview News-Journal* that on a cold November night in 1927, he was conducting the train through rural Marion County when he stopped at a telephone house to call ahead.[x] When Eason opened the door to the phone house, he caught a glimpse of something standing in the flickering firebox light of the train's oil-burning engine. He said it appeared to be "a giant ape or a gorilla . . . standing on its back feet with its arms upraised and teeth bared."[102]

Eason was so frightened he retreated back to the engine where he told the engineer and fireman what he'd seen. Not surprisingly, neither of the men wanted to get off the train to investigate.

The incidents eventually sparked an organized "monster hunt" that was conducted by locals and a few outsiders who had responded to the press coverage. In a 1965 *United Press Interna-*

---

x   Prior to the installation of modern signal and centralized traffic control systems, all communications on the line had to be done by phones stationed along the tracks.

tional article titled "Town Fed Up With Monster Hunters," Sheriff Luke Walker of Jefferson told a reporter that Bigfoot hunters from three states had overrun his small town since the news of Maples's encounter had spread.[103]

Marion County 'Monster' Recalls 1927 Experience

Additional credence to the existence of a "monster" in t h e Jefferson - Lodi area of Marion County was g i v e n Thursday morning by a 61-year-old T&P Railway conductor, Richard Eason, 1310 Timpson Street in Longview.

Eason thinks the "monster" whose giant tracks have b e e n spotted there is either a giant ape or a gorilla. He believes that he once saw either this "monster" or one of its ancestors back in 1927 on a cold November night.

Interest in the Marion County "Monster" or whatever it is continued to mount Thursday. On Wednesday, hundreds of persons — some from great distances—

visited the area where the tracks were discovered by Mrs. Herbert Manning of Jefferson. Mrs. Manning found the huge tracks measuring 5¼ inches wide by 7¼ inches long near the O l d Foundry Cemetery. She said that before she spotted them, she had just heard what she described as "a low, friendly growl" while she and a Tyler friend, Mrs. W. L. Sharp, were visiting the cemetery.

Plans were being made for a concentrated s e a r c h of t h e wooded areas where the huge footprints have been left by the "monster" over the past week. It is likely that this search will take place over the weekend.

Eason said his shattering experience with the "monster" or its ancestors occurred before the woods had been cut over in that area and the T&P Railway was just building the Payne siding between Jefferson and Lodi.

The veteran conductor said (See MONSTER, Page 2-A)

The Weather

Cloudy tonight. M o s t l y cloudy Friday; 60 per cent chance of showers Friday. Not quite so warm Friday. Low 71. High Friday 87.

Marion County Monster article from September 9, 1965

(Longview News-Journal)

Some particularly harrowing incidents involving murderous, ape-like creatures were said to have taken place in the area around the same time. The information was published in 1970 by the now defunct *Bigfoot Bulletin*. The report (which appeared in Issue #22) was submitted by Nick E. Campbell, an Army trainee stationed at Fort Ord, California. Campbell relates that two of his fellow trainees from the Texas National Guard, Private David Lawson and Private Royal Jacobs, both from Longview, Texas, told him that:

> *In or about the year 1965, there was a rash of reports of a giant hairy creature roaming the thickets and back country between Jefferson and Longview, Texas, but nearest to Longview. A man and his little daughter reported it as being large, black and not a bear. Several head of cattle and a couple of people were supposedly killed by it. Private Jacobs was a member of a posse that hunted the creature when he was a teenager. He told me that he saw the body of one of the murdered people and that the victim had been torn apart. At the time he threw his gun back in the car and went home.[104]*

Jacobs, Campbell said, was a licensed minister, and he would vouch for the truthfulness of both men. There must have been some other reports or information since the section is titled "Concerning the Longview, Texas, Reports." But as it stands, this is the only written information available regarding this rather outrageous claim. Dwain Dennis, a journalist and Jefferson resident, who interviewed Johnny Maples in 1965 said he had also looked into the story reported in the *Bigfoot Bulletin* but found no evidence that there were ever any killings in Marion County that could be attributed to Bigfoot.

While the truth of this extreme report remains a mystery, according to a growing number of witnesses there is little doubt something huge and hairy was stalking the woods of Marion over the next few decades. One of these witnesses is Brad McAndrews, a medical research biologist whose family owned a cabin in Marion County up until 1990. I have personally interviewed McAndrews and learned the scope of his family's rather harrowing experiences.

It all began in 1976 when his aunt, Amanda Green,[xi] and her family were staying at the cabin for the summer. The cabin was located on a dead-end road near Black Cypress Creek, surrounded by a cattle farm and heavy woods. One afternoon Amanda and her mother were walking near a small watering hole that had been dug out to water a new calf when they noticed several footprints in the mud surrounding it. The footprints looked human-like, yet different, and there seemed to be two sets with one being much larger than the other. Upon inspection, the women noticed that the toes seemed to be aligned straight across at the top of the ball, rather than slanted like a typical human foot. And the big toe was extremely large, not to mention one of the tracks was far too large to be a human.

The women immediately connected the strange tracks to a series of eerie howls they had heard on previous nights. These howls, or screams, seemed to be coming from the direction of the watering hole.

The women dismissed the tracks as some sort of anomaly, not knowing what to think. However, this was just the beginning. A few nights later, the family was watching television in the cabin when they noticed an extremely foul odor drifting through an open window. The smell was followed by the sound of a deep, drawn-out growl that came from right outside the window. Amanda's mother and father both jumped out of their chairs and looked out the window but saw nothing.

A few nights later, Amanda's sister was standing by the kitchen sink when she smelled the same rank odor coming through

---

xi Alias used for privacy.

the open window. She called for Amanda and her mother, who came quickly. They all agreed the smell was very distinct and unusual. None of them were willing to investigate, however. Later, the sisters were awakened by the sound of someone or something hitting on the outer wall near the kitchen. When they woke their mother, she dismissed it and told them to get back in bed.

Finally, the mystery came into frightening focus as Amanda returned one night from a neighbor's house. It was rather late, and she had driven the family's car. When she arrived at the cabin, she found that the gate to the driveway had been closed. Amanda parked the car outside the gate and waited a few moments for her eyes to adjust to the darkness of the night. She then got out and began walking to the gate. Rather than open it and pull the car inside, she decided to bend down and slip through the strands of the barbed-wire fence that extended from it on both sides. As soon as she got one leg through, she heard a "lopping sort of sound" coming toward her. Amanda hurried to get through the fence. A second later, something was looming above her, bending down as if to inspect her. She could feel the hot breath of the thing as it moved its head closer. It was dark, but Amanda could see it was some kind of animal, perhaps a bear. She began screaming as she became entangled in the wire. The animal must have been alarmed by her screaming because it stood up and started running back down the fence line. Amanda could see that it was running upright on two legs before it disappeared into the darkness. Moments later her father and mother came out of the house in response to her screams. They took her inside where she told them of the experience in frightened gasps.

A few days later, the family found the new calf dead. Its neck had been broken, and it was laying partway through the fence as if it had been dragged. Its mouth was crusted by a thick, foamy lather indicating that it had been running or in dire distress in the minutes before it was killed.

The family was quite shaken by that point, not knowing exactly what they were dealing with or how to handle the situation. Fortunately for them, the bizarre incidents suddenly stopped with no explanation. It would be more than a decade before the strange visitor returned, and this time it would be the most dramatic incident of all.

In the summer of 1989, Brad McAndrews and his brother were staying at the cabin with their grandparents and aunt. He was ten years old at the time and always enjoyed his time in the outdoors surrounding Jefferson. One afternoon, his grandmother and aunt offered to take him and his younger brother for a picnic on the property, so they ventured from the cabin and walked past an old barn searching for a good place to spread out the blanket. Remembering a good spot, McAndrews ran ahead, beyond sight of the others. When he arrived at the spot, however, he found it to be far more overgrown than he'd remembered.

As McAndrews began walking back, he heard a rustle in the woods. Something was apparently coming directly toward him. Thinking it might be a deer, he stopped a moment to see if it would cross his path. As he stood there waiting, the noise of cracking twigs and crunching leaves became louder until an animal finally emerged from the woods. But it was no deer. It was an ape-like creature seven to eight feet tall with dark, reddish-brown hair and weathered looking skin. At first it was running on all fours, but upon seeing McAndrews, it stopped and stood up on two legs.

"When it was at about nine to twelve yards from me and about two feet off of the roadway, it used a large wooden fence post to hoist itself into a bipedal progression, using its left arm and hand," McAndrews told me. "Its change in gait or posture did not result in a change in its speed. It then took a few running steps before passing behind a five-foot sapling and stopping right before me. I could hear and feel the weight of this animal as it impacted the ground. When it reached me, it immediately stopped and squared its shoulders at me. I had never been so scared in my life, even to this very day."

McAndrews stood, completely frozen and holding his breath as the huge animal stood before him. "This creature seemed to be just as startled to see me as I was to see it. His facial expression and body mannerisms told me that he was caught off guard and seemed very apprehensive as if it wasn't sure what to do. We locked eyes with each other for a number of seconds before he turned his upper torso back and to his right (as if looking over its shoulder), as if considering to take off, only to turn back to me and lock eyes again, and repeating this twice more."

As McAndrews stood transfixed on the creature, he heard his brother shout from a distance. When the animal heard the voice, it instantly sprinted off on two legs, using its hands to tunnel through the thick trees as it ran into the woods. Relieved, McAndrews ran toward his brother as fast as his legs could carry him.

"From its facial features and expression, body language, and walking/running gait, this creature was scarily human," McAndrews recalled. "I could tell that it was intelligent by the way it seemed to be assessing his circumstances."

Whatever it was stalking the woods of Marion County, it would remain a mystery. Neither McAndrews nor anyone in his family ever saw the creature again, but the experiences would remain clearly etched in their minds.

Caddo Creature

Just thirteen miles east of Jefferson lies the hauntingly picturesque Caddo Lake. This swampy lake and its network of associated bayou channels and woodlands stand as a living legacy to the primitive nature of East Texas. The landscape here is filled with briny waters, ancient cypress trees, and ghostly Spanish moss that bring to mind a primordial past rarely seen in today's world.

Caddo is one of the only natural lakes in Texas and is thought to have been formed by either the New Madrid earthquakes of 1811–1812 or as a result of a huge logjam in the Red River, which in the early 1800s forced enough water into Big Cypress Bayou to create the lake. The resulting wetlands system is comprised of about 26,800 acres of cypress swamp that boasts over two hundred bird species and countless animals including deer, raccoon, beaver, mink, nutria, hogs, squirrel, armadillo, frogs, turtles, snakes, and alligators just to name a few.

Given the prehistoric-looking landscape, it is perhaps not surprising that sightings of a Bigfoot-like creature (one I have dubbed the "Caddo Creature"[xii]) have proliferated over the years. The landscape offers plenty of sustenance and seclusion, making it possible for just about anything to live back in its shadowy recesses even today. In fact, the creature seen near the town of Jefferson could very well call Caddo Lake and its four watersheds (Little Cypress Bayou, Big Cypress Bayou, Black Cypress Bayou, and Jeems Bayou) home. I have spent many days and nights camping and canoeing along the twisting channels of the lake and can attest to its potential when it comes to Bigfoot habitat.

Legends of strange things in the area date back to the very first inhabitants. The Caddo tribe, for whom the lake was named, spoke of a race of large beings who inhabited the woods of the Ark-La-Tex (the area where Arkansas, Louisiana, and Texas meet). According to Kathy Strain, archaeologist and author of *Giants, Cannibals & Monsters: Bigfoot in Native Culture*, they referred to them as the *ha'yacatsi*, which translates to "lost giants."[105]

In modern times, I've interviewed several credible witnesses who have encountered the alleged Caddo Creature. One of

---

xii Not to be confused with the "Caddo Critter" of Caddo, Texas, three hundred miles to the west.

these was Charles Fason. Fason grew up on the west side of Caddo Lake, and as a boy he and his brother spent countless hours exploring its murky backwaters. They had their own boat and even constructed a treehouse where Big Cypress Bayou joins the main lake channel (in an area known as Devil's Elbow) to use for hunting and overnight fishing trips. One night in the summer of 1969, the Fason brothers were sleeping in their treehouse when Charles was awakened by noises around midnight. He figured it was the usual "night critters" sniffing around but decided to have a look anyway. As he peered between wooden slats of the crude treehouse wall, he was shocked to see a tall, upright animal standing a short distance away. Charles quickly awakened his brother.

"We're sitting there looking at this thing, and it started moving towards us," Fason told me. It walked to where they had thrown some leftovers from dinner and reached down to scoop them up. "Then it looked right directly back at us."

For a few tense moments the boys remained frozen, wondering what the animal would do now that it was aware of their presence. But after a few moments, it took off into the woods at an incredible speed.

"For something this big to move that fast was unbelievable," Fason recalled. "We could hear limbs snapping as it ran. Needless to say I didn't sleep the rest of the night. We were watching to see if it came back, but it never did."

The next day the brothers found several huge footprints left by the creature in the soft mud. The prints had five toes, with a uniquely larger big toe, and although they looked human, they were decidedly not. The boys did not have a ruler, but they compared the impressions to their own feet. Fason estimates the creature's foot was at least sixteen inches. Judging by the height of the treehouse and the position where the creature was standing, Fason estimated it must have stood over seven feet tall.

Fason noticed the creature had not made any verbal noises, although he and his brother had heard unusual high-pitched howls in the area on several other occasions. These mysterious calls did not come from any animal or bird they were familiar with, and after their sighting, he believed the unidentified howls may have been connected to the strange animal. The swamp could get pretty spooky at night, and this only made it spookier.

Interestingly, Fason's description of the animal's speed and movement is quite similar to what Brad McAndrews observed. Fason also noted that its footprints had an unusually large big toe. The same attribute was seen by McAndrews's aunt Amanda when she and her mother found tracks in 1976. The Fasons and McAndrewses are not acquainted, so it's remarkable they would note such specific and similar details in their stories.

In the spring of 1984, a woman was driving on Cypress Drive near the lake at around midnight when a huge, hairy creature suddenly darted across the road. The sighting was brief, but she could see that it was approximately six feet in height and covered in dark hair. It ran on two legs as it jumped a fence and vanished into the woods beyond.[106]

In the fall of 1987, a man was hunting along Big Cypress Bayou in Harrison County (not far from the Fason brothers' treehouse) when he also observed a strange animal. According to the man, he was in his deer stand around mid-afternoon when he noticed a dark figure moving approximately fifty yards away. It stood up from a crouched position in the shallow, murky water of the bayou. The animal "appeared to be six feet tall, covered with hair from head to toe."[107] As the hunter watched, the thing moved its head from side to side, as if looking for something. Then, after about two minutes, it simply turned and walked into the woods. The experience was so unnerving, the hunter decided to leave the area as quickly as he could rather than pursue the creature.

A few years later, a man experienced two strange incidents on his family's property at Caddo Lake. According to a report filed with the Texas Bigfoot Research Center, the first incident occurred sometime in 1988 while he and his wife were visiting his grandmother, who owned the property. It was dusk, and the family was sitting on the porch when they heard an unusual howl in the woods behind the house. No one, not even the grandmother who had lived there most of her life, could identify the animal. During the discussion, the man's grandmother mentioned she had lately felt as though she were "being watched" anytime she was near the woods.[108]

In December 1989, the man returned with a friend so they could deer hunt on the property. About two hours before dawn the men settled into their deer stands, spaced about one quarter mile apart. The witness (the grandson) noted that his stand was at the edge of a pipeline clearing. It was a very cold morning and nothing was moving as the man shivered in his stand. It was still dark, but a bright moon provided illumination. Finally, about an hour before the sun rose, he noticed something coming out of the woods. It was moving along the opposite side of the pipeline toward his stand, walking upright on two legs. His first thought was that it must be another hunter trespassing on the property, but he did not see a gun, nor did it look completely like a man. Despite the bipedal locomotion, it looked more animal-like.

"This thing just walked out of woods that are hard for me to walk through during the daytime without getting cut up from the briars," the witness explained. "At first it was probably 75 yards away but it was getting closer. I thought maybe I'm seeing things, but I decided to click the safety off on my gun just in case."[109]

The click of the safety was barely audible, yet immediately after the hunter clicked it, the figure turned toward him. Somehow it had heard the sound. It then began walking backward while still looking in the direction of the hunter.

"After about four steps backwards, it quickly spun around . . . took a few more steps and quickly exited the pipeline," the witness continued. At that point a tree just inside the woods began to shake violently, as if the thing was signaling a warning.

The hunter was too scared to exit his deer stand until his friend finally returned to get him. After telling him about the strange experience, the two men searched the area but found no tracks or other evidence. Once again, the woods held their secrets.

Around the same time, two men had an equally disturbing experience at the Jeems Bayou watershed on the north end of Caddo Lake. According to Roger Murray—who contacted me a few years ago—his friend Tommy had a camp there along the banks. One day Tommy and a friend drove up there on a weekday to do some work. When they pulled into the camp, they noticed what appeared to be two legs visible under a clump of leaves next to a tree about thirty yards away. Tommy put the car in park, and both men watched as the legs swayed from side to side as if the "owner" was trying to get a look at their car. Suddenly, it stepped back from the tree into the sunlight. Now the men could see it was a tall, dark, humanoid figure. Tommy said it made eye contact, and as soon as it did, the thing bolted toward the lake. It ran like a deer, instantly at full speed.

Tommy jumped out of the car and tried to chase it, but it had already disappeared into a thicket of cypress and tupelo trees. He could hear splashing footsteps as whatever it was ran into the waters of Jeems Bayou.

Tommy described it as being quite tall, perhaps seven feet, and fairly lean with skin or hair that was shiny in the sun. He surmised it was shiny because it was wet. Neither Tommy nor his friend would admit it was a "Bigfoot" per se, but they were adamant they saw something they could not explain that day. It was disturbing, to say the least.

In 1999, Eric Holley was fishing near Jeems Bayou around dusk when he thought he heard someone walking through the woods. He looked up and saw a figure moving in the trees, but it wasn't a person. It appeared to be some kind of large, hair-covered animal.

"It was big; eight-foot tall probably," Holley told Ken Gerhard and I as we interviewed him in the Jefferson General Store one afternoon. "I've seen bears before, and I knew it wasn't a bear."

The creature never looked at Holley as it passed by. It simply moved further into the woods and eventually out of sight. Holley was awestruck. He'd heard the legends of Bigfoot in East Texas but wasn't sure he believed. "Never in your wildest dreams do you think you're gonna see something like that," he told us.

His statement seems to be universal when it comes to sightings of these seemingly impossible creatures. It's as if something from a movie stepped right out into real life. Perhaps one of these did.

Boating to Devil's Elbow in Caddo Lake
(L to R: Charles Fason, Lyle Blackburn, Ken Gerhard, Tom Shirley)

(Photo by Taylor James Johnson)

Sasquatch Cinema

In addition to its history of Bigfoot encounters, Caddo Lake is also known for its role in several Bigfoot-related movies. The first and most notable of these is *Creature from Black Lake* released by Howco International Pictures in 1976. The film was actually inspired by tales of swamp-dwelling "monsters" that emanated from Jefferson and Caddo Lake, as well as the equally eerie Bayou Bodcau in nearby Louisiana. The movie was fueled by an attempt to duplicate the box office success attained by *The Legend of Boggy Creek* four years earlier. Like *The Legend of Boggy Creek*, it was an independently produced, southern-made film that reflected the burgeoning interest in Bigfoot in the 1970s.

The film's plot involves two researchers from Chicago who come to Louisiana to investigate reports of a hairy, man-like creature that allegedly haunts the banks of a nearby swamp. In the process of their investigation, the men come face to face with an angry Sasquatch that in many ways reflects the aggressive nature noted in some of the real-life encounters. The locals do not want to admit to the existence of such a creature, but in the end, even the sheriff has to deal with the reality of it as the two researchers fight for their lives.

The story is set in the small town of Oil City, Louisiana, located on the east side of Caddo Lake. The town was actually used in the film and all the swamp scenes were shot at Caddo Lake. The primordial features of Caddo make it an ideal location for a monster movie, and *Creature from Black Lake* benefits greatly from its spooky vibe. To this day, it stands as one of the best Bigfoot horror films ever made.

More recently, Caddo Lake was used as the filming location for *Boggy Creek: The Legend Is True,* released in 2010. While this movie has nothing to do with the original, it obviously draws influence from *The Legend of Boggy Creek* for its title and from *Creature from Black Lake* for its scenery. The low-budget indie,

Skookum: The Hunt for Bigfoot (2014) also used Caddo Lake as the backdrop for many of its outdoor scenes.

Creature from Black Lake one-sheet movie poster (1976)

I have even filmed there on two occasions. First, as part of the "Squatchsploitation" (2015) episode of the Animal Planet show, *Finding Bigfoot*, in which I appear alongside the cast to discuss the history of sightings in the Caddo Lake area. Then a few years ago Ken Gerhard and I investigated the Caddo Creature as part of our independently produced series, *American Monster Tour*. Once again, Caddo Lake provided the perfect backdrop for a monster tale that spans both real life and cinematic legacy. It's a truly unique place that I recommend visiting if you have a love for Bigfoot or the great outdoors.

Tracks in the Midst

While much of Bigfoot history is made up of anecdotal eyewitness reports, there is a collection of possible physical evidence to support the claims. This evidence consists of suspected hair samples, scat piles, nesting areas, handprints, and foot tracks. If these creatures are actually living, breathing entities, then it only makes sense they would leave behind some sort of biological sign. Much of the evidence collected is left to speculation, but as DNA technology advances, perhaps it will someday unlock the mystery.

Of all the suspected evidence, none has been as important to the story as the tracks. These footprint impressions, in many ways, represent the cornerstone of the phenomenon since not only do they offer a dramatic physical representation of the creature's presence, but they were also instrumental in the very naming of the creature.

It started in August 1958 when a construction worker by the name of Jerry Crew discovered dozens of huge, man-like footprints on a logging road near Bluff Creek in northern California. He and his fellow workers were perplexed, and when more tracks were found in October, the men began to refer to the mysterious track-maker as "Big Foot." Crew made a plaster cast of one of the impressions and took it to the office of the *Humboldt Times* in nearby Eureka. The editor of the paper, Andrew Genzoli, was so intrigued by the story, he published the details along with a photograph of Jerry Crew holding the cast. In the article, Genzoli referred to the creature as *Bigfoot*, and thus the name was officially on record.

As the years progressed, more "Bigfoot tracks" were discovered in California and other regions of the Pacific Northwest. Eventually tracks were found in other places across North America as the Bigfoot story gained momentum. Even at the outset of the Marion County Monster case in 1965, tracks were mentioned in the investigation.

Today, suspected tracks are still being discovered in Bigfoot hot spots around the country, and that includes Marion County. According to Danny Dupont, a personal friend who lives near Caddo Lake, he talked to a police officer who found a huge, man-like track in December 2016 about one mile north of Caddo Lake. The officer was alarmed because not only was the foot very large, but it seemed unlikely that a person would be barefoot in the remote, wooded area, especially in the dead of winter. Unfortunately the officer did not have any plaster with him to make a cast.

Several suspected tracks were found in 1994 in Cass County, just north of Marion, by a family who had also reported encounters with Bigfoot creatures on their property. Since 1990, several members of the McElmurry family had heard strange growls and howls coming from the woods surrounding their home, while some of them had also seen huge, hair-covered creatures resembling Bigfoots. This led to the discovery of several promising tracks that may have been left by the beastly visitors. Two of the best examples measured fourteen inches and eighteen inches, respectively.

The McElmurry family reported the incidents to Dr. Carl Baugh, founder of the Creation Evidence Museum in Glen Rose, Texas. Doctor Baugh, along with several of his colleagues, promptly visited the area so they could examine the tracks and otherwise investigate. During their visit, Baugh located hair samples that he suspected might belong to one the creatures. Based on the evidence and interviews with members of the family, the doctor believed there were four creatures living there: a male, two females, and a juvenile.[110] The family's property was heavily wooded and close to a lake, so there was plenty of space for such creatures to roam. There was also a prime food source. The family felt the creatures had been taking advantage of discarded chicken carcasses that were being dumped by chicken ranchers in a nearby pit. Recent development of a portion of the land, however, seemed to have reduced the activity, and by the end of 1994 things had grown quiet. No conclusive data was ever gleaned from the hair samples.

In December 2017, Shon Littlejohn was fishing in a rural area north of Caddo Lake when he noticed what looked like a large footprint in the mud. Upon closer inspection, he could clearly see toe impressions, yet the print was approximately sixteen inches in length with little evidence of a human arch. A second track was also visible stamped in the dark mud of the creek bank.

"It was like a human foot, but the toes were impressed a little deeper in the mud, and from the shape of it, you could tell it wasn't human," Littlejohn told myself and Ken Gerhard as we interviewed him at the site of the discovery. "And of course at about sixteen inches long, you know there's not going to be a human like that out here barefoot."

Littlejohn is an experienced woodsman who has hunted and fished all of his life. He's encountered all of the normal aspects of wildlife, but this was something he simply could not explain. He did not cast the tracks, but fortunately he snapped a photo.

As we've seen, tracks have been reported throughout Texas suggesting that no matter how stealthy these creatures may be, they can still leave some trace of their presence.

Photo of the track found by Shon Littlejohn in December 2017
(Photo by Shon Littlejohn)

Lakes, Pines, and More Signs

All around the Bigfoot Capital of Jefferson, the woodlands teem with tales of hairy hominids. Many of these come from the heaviest parts of the woods or around the various creeks and lakes that dot the map like jagged blue splotches. One such place is Lake of the Pines located west of Jefferson. It's another place I've visited on occasion and can attest to the abundance of tall pines and shadowy places were reclusive creatures may dwell. On one camping trip to the area in 2009, I even spotted a jaguarundi, a secretive wildcat not typically seen in East Texas. It is fairly common in Brazil, Peru, and Venezuela, and has inhabited some parts of United States, but is thought to be extinct in most U.S. locations at this point.

As far as Bigfoot, several sightings have taken place in the vicinity of Lake of the Pines. In the summer of 1976, a woman and her husband were driving toward the lake an hour before sunset when she noticed a hair-covered creature squatting down along the side of the road a mere ten to fifteen feet from their car.

"It was squatted down like a human would next to a fence post," she reported. "Even squatted down, it was as tall or taller than the fence post."[111]

The woman was rather shaken because as far as she could tell, it wasn't a human or a bear. It was facing her and she could see it clearly. As they passed, the thing turned its head and looked at her. It was a moment in time she will never forget.

An almost identical sighting occurred twenty years later only a few miles south. In 1996, Anna D. and her son were driving near Woodlawn en route to Lake of the Pines when they saw what looked like a large man wearing a brown fur coat. It was dark, but they could see the figure well enough in the headlights since it was less than ten feet from the road.

"It looked like it was kneeling, possibly on one knee facing away from us," Anna recalled. She slowed the car to look but was too apprehensive to stop.[112]

In 1985, Tony Fuller was hiking near the lake when he was also confronted with an alarming sight. In an interview I conducted several years ago, Fuller told me he was walking along an old trail at about 6:00 p.m. when he suddenly got an overwhelming feeling that something was watching him from the trees. The sensation was so strong he actually stopped walking. As he stood there listening and looking into the trees, he noticed the woods became uncomfortably quiet. To his left, a stick cracked, followed by the sound of movement. Before he could even look, a large figure darted from the woods and ran across the path in front of him. He could only see it for a few seconds, but it was enough to tell that it was something massive, moving on two legs and covered in dark brown hair. It had the shape of a very large person, but was "some kind of animal," he said. After it was gone, Fuller smelled a foul, lingering odor.

"I turned and practically ran back down the trail where I had just come from," he said. "I don't know what it was, but I never want to experience anything like that again. It still gives me chills even talking about it today."

In 1979, a family's serene Easter Sunday turned into a nightmare when they encountered a rather aggressive creature in Harrison County. According to the report, a couple and their two young girls were enjoying the afternoon on some property near Woodlawn when they heard a "loud crunching" in the brush. They could not see whatever was making the noise but were spooked enough to return to their car. At that point, the husband decided to do some target shooting with his pistol near a deep ravine. According to the woman: "We shot several times when suddenly, a large animal lunged into the ravine in front of us only about 10 to 15 feet. He paused, looked at us and then in one leap, jumped out of [the] ravine. We froze for a moment then [my] husband grabbed our six-year-old and I took the hand of the nine-year-old. We ran towards the car."[113]

They could hear the animal pursuing them as it crashed through the surrounding brush, but it stopped before they reached the car. She described the animal as being grayish in color, covered in hair five to six inches long, under which they could still see skin. It had wide shoulders, long arms, and was "powerful looking." She added that: "Unlike the drawings of Bigfoot, he had a short neck and round head. Far more human looking than the blocky thick shapes of the drawings."

The frightened family promptly fled the scene in their car. The aggressive nature of the creature harkened back to the incident in 1965 when Johnny Maples was chased down a road in Jefferson.

The *Bigfoot Casebook* includes an incident said to have occurred in Marshall in 2001. In this case a hunter was putting out apples to attract deer. When he returned to hunt at the baiting area, he was shocked to see "an ape-like creature holding the hindquarter of a deer."[114] Once again, deer seem to be a meal choice for the creatures.

As we move further from Jefferson, radiating out in all directions, it's not hard to find a sighting report or whispers among the locals about the elusive creature that haunts this section of the Piney Woods. Avinger, Diana, Linden, Harleton—it doesn't matter where the pin falls, it's likely to be on target.

I corresponded with a witness who had a very close encounter outside of Longview in July 1975. Steven Brooks told me he had set out to fish along the upper part of the Sabine River one morning. He had parked under an overpass bridge just before sunrise and as he was walking toward the river with his pole and tackle box, he noticed what looked like a large person squatting down near the water. As he got closer in the dim light, he realized it was actually a huge, hairy animal. It was looking in the opposite direction and did not notice Brooks until he got within ten feet. Needless to say, Brooks abandoned his plans for fishing that day.

The community of Hallsville, between Longview and Marshall, is another place familiar with the stories. An article that ran in the November 28, 1976 (a year that seems to keep coming up!) issue of the *Longview News-Journal*, asked: "Do [Bigfoot] creatures lurk in the East Texas creek bottoms?" In the article, reporter Charles Able recounted an incident in which a woman had been frightened by a Bigfoot in a blackberry patch near Hallsville. She said, "The animal came from the bushes, breaking trees and bushes in his rush."[115]

The incident was investigated by Zollie Owens, a man who began researching the Texas phenomenon long before it was popular. Owens claimed that on one occasion he had placed some food on a local man's farm in attempt to lure in the creature. Sure enough, he said the creature eventually showed up, walking from the woods into a clearing.

"The creature walked upright and was covered with silver hair," Owens told the reporter. "With him was a smaller, obviously female creature with red-tinged hair. The larger of the two seemed protective of the other."

Owens estimated the larger one's height at around twelve feet, which is at the top end of the typical height estimations for Bigfoot. If this is the case, it was surely a native of Texas, where everything is always bigger.

An old stagecoach road through the woods
outside the town of Marshall, Texas

(Photo by Lyle Blackburn)

7.

SABINE THINGS

Moving southward along the eastern border of Texas, the Piney Woods seem to grow taller and thicker as the evergreens cast long shadows across an ever-increasing network of rivers, swampy bottomlands, and tangled brush where the mosquitoes grow to record size. It's a land marked by miles of barbed-wire fences that protect a seemingly infinite row of woodlands where it's hard to tell one property from the next.

Among the rusted wire and endless trees, the Sabine River cuts a decisive path. The river, which originates in the prairies of North Texas, is an extremely long waterway that eventually forms much of the boundary between Texas and Louisiana as it snakes through miles of the lower Piney Woods and western bayou country. This is an area of abundant rainfall, and the Sabine discharges the largest volume of any river in Texas. The name of the Sabine River (*Río de Sabinas*) comes from the Spanish word for cypress due to the numerous bald cypresses growing along the lower river. The waterway is revered by campers, hikers, and paddlers alike for its tranquil beauty, but to people like me, it's also notable for the presence of a legendary Bigfoot the locals refer to as the "Sabine Thing."

Dramatic sightings of the alleged beast date back many years and, given the environment, it makes perfect sense. It's the farthest point from the arid flats of El Paso and what most would consider prime habitat for anything that prefers deep woods and dark waters. I've spent time canoeing down a good stretch of the river, and it's not hard to imagine that a population of reclusive creatures could make a suitable home here. It is Texas nature at its finest, yet it can be quite spooky. When the sun sets and mysterious howls begin to echo from the bottoms, it is best to prepare for the unexpected.

Panola Phenomenon

James Lawson was not the sort of man who feared any aspect of the Sabine River Bottoms. He'd grown up in Panola County and spent a good portion of his younger days hunting, fishing, and camping along the river there. He lived in Tatum, but often visited the area east of Carthage around what the locals call Hills Lake.[xiii]

Lawson's grandmother, who was born in 1899, had lived her entire life in those bottoms. She would often warn young James about a mysterious creature the family called a "Wooly Booger." She claimed that one of her sisters had been abducted by this thing and was never seen again. In fact, her sister *had* gone missing at the age of twenty-two after heading off into the woods to pick leaves for what Southerners call "poke salad."[xiv]

Lawson never paid much heed to the story of the Wooly Booger, figuring it was just something made up to scare kids or to explain away the tragic disappearance of his grandmother's sister. However, that would all change one day in 1979 as he and his father were fishing on Hills Lake. In a detailed correspondence, Lawson told me:

> *[We] had put the jon boat in at dawn and worked our way to the most secluded part of the lake, very quietly fishing the edges with cane poles. I was in the front, facing my father as he paddled very quietly without removing the paddle, just swirling it softly. As God is my witness, I saw him turn white as a sheet. As I looked at him, he pointed toward the bank behind me. I slowly turned to*

---

xiii My father's family is from Carthage, and as a child we often visited my great-grandmother, Pearl Shaw, at her home there. Pearl lived to the amazing age of 106!

xiv Poke salad (or poke sallet) is a dish made from the slightly less toxic leaves of a kudzu-like plant called *Phytolacca americana*. It is a regional cuisine popular in Appalachia and the American South.

> *look. There, a few feet from the water's edge, I saw what I first thought was a huge black bear sitting on a log facing away from us. It looked as if it was digging in the leaf matter and had its back to us. As I said out loud, 'bear?' the creature turned its head and saw us, stood up on two legs and walked off very swiftly. When my father saw this he quickly turned the bow around, and paddling as fast as he could, took us to the other end of the lake. We loaded the boat back onto his pickup and left. All the way home we didn't speak (which was not unusual). [After we arrived home] my father told me that the 'bear' was not a bear and for me to never—and he meant never—speak of it again. He said it was bad luck to have seen it, and more so to tell of seeing it.*

It was an experience that left Lawson with little doubt that something monstrous *was* living in deepest reaches of the Sabine.

Ten years before Lawson's scare, young Teresa Dixon, her aunt, and her younger sister were exploring the woods behind her grandmother's house near Beckville in Panola County when they saw something they would never forget. It was the winter of 1969, and there had been a fire in the woods. The girls were curious to see where it had burned, so they ventured over their grandmother's barbed-wire fence and headed out in search of the spot.

As the girls were walking, they noticed some kind of animal crouching behind a tree. As soon as they made eye contact, it stood up on two legs. It was similar to a human yet covered in what looked like brown hair.

"It was very tall, thin, and hairy like an ape, but was more man-like," Dixon told me in an interview. She's unsure of the exact distance they were from the creature, but distinctly remembers seeing its eyes. "It didn't look menacing," she recalled. "And it wasn't scared."

Maybe not, but the girls were certainly scared. Enough that they turned and ran as fast as they could back to their grandmother's house through a big field and over the barbed-wire fence. "I don't remember how I got over that fence," Dixon said, "but I'll never forget what I saw that day."

After telling her family of the experience, her grandfather admitted that he'd seen a similar creature several years before near their house. He said he kept it quiet so as not to frighten anyone.

Approximately two years after Dixon's sighting, around 1971, her uncle claimed to have seen the creature (or one like it) while camping in the bottoms between Beckville and Carthage. Other locals whispered of a strange beast responsible for many unexplained livestock deaths.

In 1986, my friend Jeff Stewart was camping in Panola County with friends as they often did on weekends. He was fifteen at the time and already a skilled outdoorsman, having grown up in a culture of hunting and fishing typical of that area. The spot where they camped was located on more than five hundred heavily wooded acres owned by his family, of which he was intimately familiar both in terms of geography and wildlife . . . or so he thought.

Earlier in the day he and his friends had caught a load of catfish in the river and cleaned them at an old pump-well present on the property. Afterward, they intentionally threw the entrails on the ground so they could return at night with flashlights to harvest any fur-bearing animals caught eating the scraps. Stewart had done this plenty of times in the past with successful results.

Later that night, after eating their fill of fish, Stewart was volunteered to go check the trap. Chiding his friends for being lazy, he grabbed his flashlight and .22 caliber rifle and headed off down the trail. As he approached the spot, he could see something there eating, dimly illuminated in the beam of his old two-cell bulb. It was rather large and hairy, so he assumed it was a hog.

However, when Stewart got within twenty yards, the thing stood up on two legs.

"I never will forget," Stewart told me during one of several conversations we've had about the event. "It never made a gesture. It just looked me dead in the face."

His first thought was that someone must be playing a joke on him—perhaps one of his friends. He even called out to it, indicating he wasn't falling for the ruse. But the more he looked at the silent figure standing before him, the more he realized it was not a person in a costume—if it was even a person at all. He had heard stories about people living down in the river bottoms who had gone feral; people who had gone down there to live and were rarely seen again. But this looked more like an animal. It was beastly despite its anthropomorphic physique.

Stewart said it was approximately five feet tall and covered in hair matted down with a layer of gray, gumbo mud from the river bottom. The face was exposed, with very dark, oily, and weathered skin that reminded him of an Australian Aborigine. It had dark eyes and a nose that was wide and almost ape-like, but still within human parameters.

Unsure of what the creature might do, Stewart leveled his gun at it. But he didn't have to pull the trigger. Seconds later the creature took three steps backward. "When it got to the edge of the bushes, where there was a pine thicket, it was still looking at me, and it just kind of disappeared backwards into the brush," Stewart explained.

After it was out of sight, the stunned teenager ran back to camp where he told his friends about the encounter. Stewart was outwardly shaken, but they still dismissed his story with a laugh, thinking perhaps he was trying to scare them. Realizing it would be hard to convince anyone he'd truly seen such a thing, he resolved to stay quiet for many years. Now, as the stories are gathered in one place, it's evident Stewart is not alone.

Not far from the location of Stewart's encounter, two hunters reportedly shot at such a creature in November 2001. According to my colleague, Jerry Hestand, both were hunting at separate locations near the Sabine River when they saw a "large ape-man" step from the trees. In both cases, the creature began walking toward the hunter. This frightened the men enough to raise their rifles and shoot. In both cases they believed to have hit the creature, yet it simply moved back into the thicket and disappeared into its shadows.

In April 2006, two men were bowfishing on the Sabine River in Panola County when they saw a similar, unexplainable creature. At around 3:00 p.m. on a clear day, they were floating along in their boat when they caught sight of a large, dark figure moving just off the bank some distance ahead. As they drifted closer, they could see that it was walking on two legs through the trees with its back toward them. The thing seemed unaware of their presence as they watched it for several tense minutes. It appeared to be at least seven feet tall and covered in dark brown hair approximately two or three inches long, with longer, darker hair on its head. It was bulky and definitely walking upright as it slowly moved away from the stunned fisherman.

One of the witnesses told my colleague John Morley that he was uncertain what the thing might have done if it had seen them, and that was the most unnerving aspect of the experience. After it disappeared from sight, his partner started the trolling motor and began to head back upstream. As soon as they felt safe, he cranked up the outboard motor and they sped to the boat ramp. Whatever it was, they did not want to see it again.[116]

On December 8, 2009, a nurse was driving near the Murvaul Creek bottoms in Panola at about 5:15 a.m. when she came upon a tall, bipedal figure in the road. It was a dark morning and slightly foggy as her headlights illuminated the unexpected figure, who appeared to be in the process of crossing the thoroughfare.

She was driving slowly at about 35 mph. She braked to avoid hitting it. The awestruck nurse continued to drive slowly by as she watched the thing walk the rest of the way across the road and head toward the woods.

In an interview with my friend Ken Stewart of the North American Wood Ape Research Conservancy (NAWAC), she said "the large subject appeared to be completely covered with one shade of hair, either dark brown or black hair [that] appeared to be of similar length all over the body. The shoulders and head were slightly stooped forward while walking. It had a thick chest and long arms and walked upright the entire time."[117]

The thick woods of Panola County
(Photo by Lyle Blackburn)

Stewart assessed the witness to be exceptionally credible and observant due to her training as a nurse. After visiting the sighting location with her, he had little doubt she saw what she said she saw that morning on the lonely stretch of road. Perhaps it was a rare glimpse of what the locals call the Sabine Thing.

The Hog Hunter

One of the most detailed and perhaps disturbing stories involving a Texas Bigfoot originates from the southern end of Panola County. The story may be familiar to many of my readers since it was featured at the beginning of my 2014 book, *Beyond Boggy Creek: In Search of the Southern Sasquatch*. It may also be familiar due to its proliferation on various blogs and videos created by other writers and researchers.

The reason for this proliferation is undoubtedly because it is one of the most dramatic and lengthy observations of an alleged Bigfoot creature to date. The fact that it happened in Texas makes it relevant and worth repeating here, of course, as well as the fact that I spoke to the witness directly. What follows is derived directly from my conversations with him.

In the early morning hours of March 2003, Paul Matlock and his cousin set out for a day of hog hunting along the Sabine River north of Joaquin. Around 4:30 a.m. they lowered their jon boat into the murky waters of the Sabine and began to motor upstream to a location where Matlock planned to hunt. When they neared the spot, Matlock's cousin nudged the craft up to the west bank and paused long enough for Paul to grab his rifle and a bag of food scraps and step out of the boat. His cousin then backed up and continued upstream to his own hunting site.

As the motor's hum faded into the darkness, Matlock used his flashlight to locate a tree stand he'd already placed there. Before ascending, he scattered a bag of apple slices and potatoes in a clearing about twenty yards away. He then climbed twenty-five feet up, donned a mosquito head net, and settled in for the wait. It was now around 5:00 a.m.

When the sun finally crept over the horizon, Matlock began to hear the distinctive sound of hogs. It was faint at first but gradually got louder as the animals worked their way toward the hunter. Finally, he spotted five of them forty-five degrees to his left and about fifty yards away. They were approaching his bait area.

While waiting for a clear shot, Matlock caught a glimpse of something else moving between the trees thirty yards to the right of the hogs. He raised his rifle to get a better look through his scope. At first he could only see the side of a dark face peering out from behind a leafless tree, but after a few moments the thing stood up and moved to another tree. Now the hunter could see it was some sort of hairy creature standing upright on two legs. It didn't look like any animal he'd seen before, and it didn't appear to be another hunter . . . even one in a ghillie suit. In fact, it didn't look like a person at all. Matlock had been hunting those woods since he was a teenager and had never seen anything like it.

Despite a growing sense of alarm, Matlock turned the scope up to maximum power and trained it on the animal as it worked from one tree to another. Each time, the creature would crouch down on all fours and leap to the next tree, where it would land at the base and stand up. It would then study the hogs intently before moving again. Its every movement was fluid and completely silent.

As the creature maneuvered closer to the hogs, Matlock studied its features. It appeared to be six to seven feet tall with a thick coat of reddish-brown hair covering most of its body except for the hands, feet, and part of the face. The face itself looked human-like with dark brown eyes and small ears. The body was very heavily built and had breasts. Apparently it was a female. Whatever the hell it was, Matlock was in shock.

The stalking continued for several more minutes until the five hogs were less than thirty yards from Matlock. Then, all at once, the thing crouched on all fours, curled its knuckles, and leaped toward its prey. As soon as it hit the ground, it let out a blood-curdling scream that pierced the morning air. The hogs panicked and scattered, but it was too late. Within two leaps the creature had descended upon them, slapping one hog so hard on its side it flew through the air and slammed into a nearby tree. When the squealing pig hit the ground, the creature leaped on it, first grabbing its neck with the right hand and then pummeling it with the huge fist of its left hand. Matlock could hear ribs cracking with every hit.

The remaining four hogs bolted into the woods. By the time their squeals faded, their brethren lay dead at the hands of the creature who then scooped it up under one arm as if it were no more than a pillow sack. The thing let out a series of whooping sounds, which were immediately answered by shorter whoops from an unseen animal deeper in the woods.

Matlock watched in fear and disbelief. It was only when the creature began to walk off that he felt any sense of relief. But it was short-lived. Without warning the creature dropped the hog to the ground and turned its head in the direction of his tree stand. At first it looked past the hunter with its eyes scanning at ground level. Then it tilted its head upward and followed the tree trunk until its eyes focused on him. Matlock managed to keep the gun trained on it, but by then he knew he did not have enough firepower. If he missed or the shot didn't take the thing down, he would surely suffer the same fate as the hapless hog.

The beast studied the hunter intently for a few moments, moving its head slightly as it did, while at the same time opening its mouth to reveal a set of yellowed teeth. Then suddenly, as if it were satisfied, the creature bent down to retrieve the hog, tucked it under its arm, and casually walked off.

Matlock watched through his trembling scope until he could no longer see the animal, then he slowly lowered the rifle and exhaled. He sat there for approximately thirty more minutes trying to calm himself down. Ultimately, he decided if the creature would have wanted to hurt him, it could have. It had not been the least bit afraid of five 150-pound-plus hogs with razor-sharp tusks, so what did it have to fear from him unless, of course, it was aware of the power of guns? But how could it? Questions railed through his mind like a locomotive.

Matlock finally crawled down from the tree and made his way back to the rendezvous point at the river's edge. In a short time his cousin motored up and stopped the engine. As the boat floated to rest on the bank, he could see that his fellow hunter was pale and shaken.

"What happened?" his cousin asked. "I heard some whooping sounds down this way."

Matlock nodded. For a moment he hesitated, but finally—reluctantly—told him what he'd witnessed, fully expecting laughter when he was done.

But there was no ridicule. His cousin merely looked him in the eye and said: "It's real. I've seen it too."

When Matlock's cousin explained that he had not only previously seen a reddish-brown creature of the same description, but also a larger one with white hair, Matlock felt a twisted sense of relief. While on one hand there were apparently huge, unknown creatures stalking his local woods, at least he wasn't crazy. His cousin admitted he had also been reluctant to tell anyone because of the same reservations. But now that they had both seen the creature, they could speak freely.

As they talked, the two men walked back to the site where the hog had been killed. Perhaps they could find footprints or other evidence. When they arrived, they found the hog's blood on the tree and ground, but unfortunately no discernable prints of the creature could be seen. A solid layer of leaves just didn't provide the conditions necessary for such remnants.

Still shaken but at least able to deal with the reality of

the encounter, Matlock followed his cousin back to the boat. He wasn't sure if he'd been lucky to see one of these creatures or profoundly unlucky, but he was sure that hunting on the southern Sabine River would never be the same again.

"Let's put it this way . . . I will never go in the woods again without feeling on edge," Matlock told me as he concluded the story. "It's not something you forget."

Upon listening to the details and questioning him at length, I could find no justifiable reason to dismiss his testimony. It was something that seemed to have had a profound effect on him. "The place where that is can only be accessed by the river," Matlock explained. "It's government land, but you won't find it on any of the state Wildlife Management Area maps. I think there might be a family of these things living up there."

If there is a family of these things living along the Sabine, the aforementioned giant mosquitoes may be the least of our worries.

The lower Sabine River
(Photo by Lyle Blackburn)

Something Is Out There

As the Sabine River flows southward, it forms the seventy-mile-long Toledo Bend Reservoir, with the Sabine National Forest along its western bank. Here, too, we find tales of Sabine Things dating back many years. In the late 1970s, a man was said to be fishing in the reservoir close to the western shore when a rank odor began to permeate the air. A few minutes later he noticed what appeared to be a person crouching behind a tree watching him. The fisherman thought it was odd, so he kept an eye on the subject for several minutes. Finally, the "person" stood up, walked into the open, and looked directly at the boat. At that point, the fisherman could see it was not a person, but instead some kind of creature that stood at least eight feet tall and was covered in reddish-brown hair. After peering at the boat, the thing turned and walked slowly up the bank and into the heavier woods above it.[118]

In November 1978, Jack M. was hunting coyote in the Sabine River Bottoms with several other men when something crossed the headlights of their truck as they drove along a dirt road. It looked like a "large animal/man-like creature covered in what appeared to thick hair" walking on two legs. It was tall, perhaps seven feet in height and possibly four hundred pounds. It crossed the road and entered the trees on the other side.[119]

The hunters were shocked. They were on a dirt trail that led from the county road alongside the river and into the bottoms about a mile down. It was very isolated and quite spooky. Hoping to catch the bizarre animal, the driver stopped the truck, and the men jumped out. They had several Bluetick and Redbone hunting dogs in the back, which they quickly turned loose. The dogs ran into the woods in the direction of the animal but returned a short time later, cowering under the protection of the truck.

The next day, Jack returned to the area with two friends to look for any signs of the thing he had seen the night before. They found a set of unusual man-like footprints and followed them through the brush down to the river, where it appeared the animal had stepped into the water and eventually came out on a log and crossed a fence. The men continued to search for the thing the rest of the day, but never caught up to it.

A few days later, a local newspaper (name unknown) ran a story about a woman who claimed to have seen "something non-human staring at her as she attempted to change a flat tire."[120] It mentioned that some local ranchers had seen more than one of these man-like creatures stealing feed from their cattle. Another woman, who lived in the river bottoms, claimed to have observed more than one of the creatures eating from her garden by moonlight. The Sabine Things seemed to be common knowledge among the locals, though so far no one has been able to catch one.

Further south in Newton County, three hunters saw something fitting the description of the Sabine Thing in July 1998. A man who I will call "B. J." said that he was with his father and a friend scouting locations for deer stands in the bottoms when they heard an eerie scream.[121] It was so startling the men literally stopped in their tracks. After a few moments without any further sound, they discussed what kind of animal it could have been, but they had no answers. Eventually they continued on, but not without the distinct feeling that something was watching them.

After approximately fifteen minutes, B. J.'s father stopped abruptly and whispered: "What the hell is that thing?!" B. J. looked up to see a large, dark figure step out from behind a clump of trees. The thing appeared to be at least eight feet tall with dark, brownish hair covering its entire body. Its head was slightly conical in shape, and it was decidedly ape-like in appearance. The three men watched as the creature turned and headed back into the trees, walking on two legs. They were at a loss to identify the animal but were absolutely sure it wasn't a bear.

Four Newton County deputies were faced with a similar

question when they witnessed an unidentified creature in 2017. According to the *Jasper Newsboy* (the oldest continuously published weekly newspaper in Texas), the Newton County Sheriff's Office received a frantic 911 call at around 1:45 a.m. from a woman who lived just southwest of the river.[122] The woman, a seventy-six-year-old widow who had lived in Newton County all of her life, said she was sleeping soundly when she was awakened by a terrible commotion on her back porch. It sounded like someone breaking into the house.

"I was there in the office when the call came in," one of the deputies explained to the Jasper reporter. "And when you hear a call like that, one with true fear on the other end of the line, you go and you get there fast. She was truly scared to death."

The call was so urgent that four deputies were dispatched to the home, located at the end of a dirt road in a very rural area. When they arrived, they found the frightened woman waiting anxiously. She told the officers she was awakened by a loud crash coming from her screened-in porch at the back of the house. The noise had stopped, but she was too afraid to go back there to see what had happened.

As the officers were listening to her story, a loud crash sounded again from the back porch. The deputies quickly launched into action, moving cautiously to the back of the house. When they got to the area of the screened-in porch, they opened the door and looked out.

"It was like someone had literally gone through that porch and tore it apart," one of the deputies said. "Chairs had been over turned [*sic*], the screen ripped open and even the door frame that led outside was ripped off the hinges and thrown about ten feet. We had no idea what we were dealing with. Our first consensus was that we had an attempted burglary and a vandalizing incident which in some ways I guess you could say it was."

The officers continued through the porch and walked into

the backyard. It was adjacent to a heavily wooded area. They initially scanned the perimeter but did not see anyone. As they continued their search, however, all of the deputies heard what they described as a "large man walking fast" in the woods.

With guns drawn and flashlights focused, they headed toward the sound fully expecting to see the perpetrator. However, what they saw is something that none of them can explain to this day.

"I have to tell you that I am not crazy," one of the deputies began. "But we all saw the same thing. It was an animal or '*something*' that stood at least eight feet tall. It was covered in hair and moved fast."

The lawmen watched as the hair-covered creature ran across the wooded area in an upright, bipedal fashion, just as a human would. It was breaking limbs as it proceeded toward a nearby creek.

"We couldn't see him as he neared the creek but we heard the splashing as he crossed it and the thing had to be moving at a high speed," the deputy said. "I have thought about this for a long time and I just cannot come up with a rational explanation for what we saw. I have been faced against hardened criminals, people who have no respect for human life, people with guns that want to harm others and I know how to handle it but this; this is something I can't process because I honestly don't know what I saw other than a creature that I can't explain."

The thing ran out of sight and the officers declined to pursue it into the dark woods. At that point, they returned to the house and attempted to calm the frightened woman. They did not tell the woman exactly what they had seen because they feared it would frighten her even more—not to mention they were simply at a loss for words to explain it.

"So, basically we waited with her until the break of dawn to make sure it didn't return and explained to her that we were not sure what had taken place but that she was safe and that was the most important thing," the lead deputy told the reporter. "None of us knew what to say. We still don't know what to say."

And that is a common reaction whether the witness is a hunter, hiker, frightened resident, or astonished lawman. Something is out there, but what it truly is remains yet unknown. Perhaps a photo would shed some light on the mysterious subject.

The author exploring the woods of East Texas

(Photo by Ashley Cheree)

Port Neches Photo

In February 2013, I was suddenly bombarded with messages informing me that "Bigfoot" had been photographed in Texas. Some of the messages came from relatives and friends that wouldn't normally have heard about such things. Apparently the alleged photo had gone viral, and I was to be informed of the matter over the course of the next week on an hourly basis.

The photograph was part of a breaking news story published February 19, 2013, by *The Port Arthur News*. A man had come to the newspaper claiming to have taken a photo of two Bigfoots along the Neches River (at the tip end of the Sabine River where it drains to the Gulf of Mexico). David Arceneaux, who took the photo, said he was cleaning graves in the Oak Bluff Cemetery at Block Bayou when he got the "fright of his life."[123]

It was a windless, overcast day in December 2012 and he was working among the headstones, cleaning off debris as he did every month. Suddenly, a howling scream came from a small strip of woods located across a bayou channel.

"I heard a blood curdling scream and a lady nearby asked me if I was OK. I told her it wasn't me," Arceneaux explained to the reporter. "We walked over to the water and looked to the left then straight ahead."

There, in the grassy area beyond the bayou, he saw what appeared to be two Bigfoot creatures. One was standing next to a tree with its arms around the trunk and the other was squatted down. Arceneaux said they had been throwing rocks in the water. The squatting creature stood up on two legs as it caught sight of the onlookers. It appeared to be least eight feet tall. Arceneaux quickly pulled out his cell phone and snapped a photo of the creatures as they stood at the edge of the wood line about one hundred yards away.

"All of a sudden they started walking then running through the woods," he continued. They were moving upright on two legs.

"When they began to run, the lady said, 'I'm leaving' and left. I stayed a few more seconds and then thought there may be a way for them to cross here so I left, scared."

Arceneaux said the creatures were covered in hair "from the mouth down like a man," and when one of them turned around he could see "hair hanging down from its arm." Arceneaux claimed he could also see the face of the creature "clear as day."

Arceneaux spoke to a game warden about the situation who told him there had been other sightings along the Neches River. He did not immediately go public with news of the photo, fearing that people would ridicule him. Later, after watching a network television show about Bigfoot, Arceneaux decided to take his story, and photo, to the press.

The photograph in question looks typical of Bigfoot photos in that it's taken from a distance and does not offer enough clarity to either confirm or deny that an unknown creature is indeed present in the snapshot. There are two dark shapes at the edge of the woods that appear to fit the profile of a Bigfoot, but they blend in with the wooded backdrop making it hard to discern very much detail. (This photographic scenario is often referred to as a "Blobsquatch" by Bigfoot researchers.) Some may argue these are simply dark blobs created by a trick of light and shadow, but there does appear to be something there that is not merely illusion.

When the news feature was posted on the internet, it quickly went viral, as these sorts of photos tend to do. Researchers began to debate the validity of the story and photo, while a mass of casual enthusiasts took it at face value. Arceneaux's photo is interesting, however, it still leaves much to be desired in terms of quality evidence, both in terms of the grainy, distant snapshot and in terms of the story.

The first issue is the geographic location. Though it is at the southern end of the Sabine watershed, along which we've already established a long history of Bigfoot sightings, the location of the cemetery is surrounded on three sides by populated, urban areas. The only way a Bigfoot could get to the location without strolling through the city would be to swim across the Neches River. It seems unlikely that such creatures would choose to swim and potentially trap themselves between water and humans.

The second issue is the location of the alleged creatures themselves within the photograph. Arceneaux claimed they were throwing rocks in the water, yet when he turned and spotted them, they were standing at the tree line perhaps a hundred yards from the edge of bayou channel. This fits with his statement that one of them was "hugging a tree" but not with the notion they were tossing rocks into the water. Not to mention the grassy area along the channel doesn't appear to be a place where very many rocks could be found.

The Neches River
(Photo by Glenn Haskins)

A final, major issue is that the so-called subjects in the film are not extremely clear and could simply be trees, stumps, or shadows that look like Bigfoot. There is just not enough clarity to say one way or another.

The validity of the photo and the debate surrounding it represents the question of Bigfoot photos in general. Are these truly capturing images of the elusive creatures or are they a form of pareidolia that forces our mind to recognize forms that are not really there? Until such time as someone gets a clear, close photograph, this will remain a key debate in the mystery.

Worth the Pursuit

On August 20, 2000, Chester Moore, Jr., along with his father, Chester Moore, Sr. and Bigfoot investigator, Bobby Hamilton, were packing up their truck after a long night in the woods of Southeast Texas when a low grunt sounded from a thicket forty yards away. The men had spent the better part of the night sitting between a creek bottom and a pine thicket while investigating an area where Bigfoot sightings had been reported as far back as the 1970s. Up until that point, the night had been uneventful with only a few faint animal calls echoing in the distance. When they heard the grunt, however, things suddenly got interesting.

Moore made a grunt in response. Surprisingly, the unseen animal grunted back. Moore grunted again, twice this time. The animal grunted twice. Whatever it was, it was responding to Moore's communication in a seemingly intelligent manner.

The three men considered going into the brush to flush the thing out, but they quickly reconsidered when another low growl sounded behind it. There was apparently two of the creatures.

Moore decided to grunt again.

"I finally grunted three times and the thing went into a

frenzy," Moore told me. "Starting with a low gurgling sound, it built itself to a higher pitch and then it let out the exact yell heard through *The Legend of Boggy Creek*." Like myself and many other Bigfoot enthusiasts, Moore is intimately familiar with the iconic howl of the creature portrayed in the classic film. It's one thing to hear such an eerie howl in the context of a movie, but to hear it in real life while in the dark woods is a completely different experience . . . one that sent chills up the spines of all three men.

"One of us said 'It's the Fouke Monster!' as the creature moved through the brush, snapped branches, and left us," Moore explained. "I don't' know if it was my communicating with it or the light from a million-candle power Q-Beam that did the job, but this thing decided it had better retreat."

Though Moore and his companions never saw the animals, they could only assume that they were perhaps the very same Bigfoot creatures said to roam the Sabine River Bottoms and beyond. And it wasn't the first time Moore had heard such a thing. While hunting rabbits with his father in Newton County at the age of eleven, an enraged cacophony of growls, yells, and grunts suddenly broke the night's silence.

"The sounds were guttural and vile and they pierced my 11-year-old soul," Moore recalled of that night. "Although it is impossible to accurately describe them in print, the sounds still echo in my mind as if I were standing behind dad right now, wondering what we had gotten ourselves into."

Moore's father, a seasoned woodsman and hunter, seemed concerned but passed it off as one of their uncle's bulls caught in a fence. Young Chester didn't believe this sounded anything like a bull and wondered why they weren't going to help the animal even if it were but didn't question his father's decision to quickly leave the area. His father later said it was a black bear, but even that explanation didn't hold up over time. Moore later worked with three captive black bears, and their sounds were nothing like what he and his father had heard on that night when he was young.

Chester Moore has since pursued a successful career as a wildlife journalist and animal conservationist, which has put him in contact with numerous wild and exotic animals and countless situations in the woods of Texas. The noise that he and the others heard in 2000 was absolutely unique and one that he suspected may belong to the mysterious, primate-like animals reported on so many occasions in the Piney Woods. He could also compare it to a real-life encounter with a known primate.

"Just nine months earlier, I encountered a howler monkey while fishing on Venezuela's Lake Guri," he said. "My guide and interpreter called the monkey a 'mono vil' or 'mean monkey,' and after messing with one of the creatures, it is easy to understand why. As we approached more closely, it jumped from branch to branch, snapping limbs and increasing the intensity of its yells. Finally, I decided to do a series of grunts to see how the animal would respond. I would grunt and it would grunt. I would grunt twice, and it would grunt twice. And finally, tired of my harassment, the monkey let out a loud roar and disappeared into the dense canopy of the South American rainforest. The fact I had previously encountered a wild primate doing the same type of thing let me know this was the real deal. It was like we were in our own version of *The Legend of Boggy Creek* and just had a mix-up with the monster."

As a professional wildlife journalist, Moore has a balanced perspective on the possibility that some kind of unknown creature could be existing not only in the wilds of Texas but in other parts of the United States. It's a notion that many wildlife professionals may dismiss, but not Moore. He has spent a good many years investigating the phenomenon, and when combined with his vast knowledge and experience with wildlife, he remains steadfast in his conclusion.

"I have never seen anything that gave me the kind of inspiration to enter such a deep, and at times, unusual pursuit," Moore said. "But I certainly heard something that made me believe there's something out there. Just what that is, however, remains elusive."

The Legend of Boggy Creek one-sheet movie poster (1972)

8.

BIG THICKET BEASTS

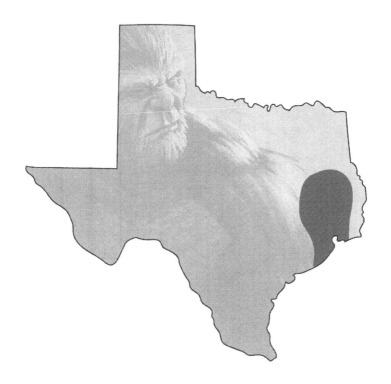

I cursed the greenbriers as I pivoted to free my camo pants from their needlelike grip. I appeared to be engaged in a bizarre dance as I continually pivoted, dodged, and jumped to avoid the annoying vines that spread like prickly tendrils over the grounds of the Sam Houston National Forest. But it was worth the effort.

On July 23, 2010, I found myself accompanying several members of the Texas Bigfoot Research Conservancy as they hiked to a site about a mile into the woods where members Michael Mayes and Daryl Colyer had previously found some unusual tracks in the soft sand of a dry creek bed. By now the tracks would have surely faded, but it was worth a return trek to the location in case more tracks had been left, or even better, we might get a glimpse of the mysterious track-maker.

Mayes and Colyer had come across the tracks by chance six weeks earlier as they were searching the area for signs of wood apes (a.k.a. Bigfoot) and scouting for potential places to leave game cameras for the purpose of capturing one on film. While hiking through the spring-bloomed forest, the duo came upon a winding creek whose waters had cut a trench ten feet deep through the woods. The creek was mostly waterless at the time yet had a moist, sand-covered floor that ran for a good distance. It appeared to be an excellent corridor of travel for anyone or any*thing* that wanted to avoid the resistant briars I was currently cursing. The fact that it was sunken below ground level also made it desirably secluded.

Upon entering the creek bed, Mayes and Colyer found wildlife tracks confirming that raccoons, opossums, deer, coyotes, and other animals had indeed used it as a convenient route of travel. The men proceeded to walk the creek looking for more signs, including those of Bigfoot. It was an area rich with sightings, so who knew what they might find. As luck would have it (which is not too often in this pursuit), they rounded a bend and found themselves looking at "numerous impressions that resembled footprints."[124] They were shocked. There appeared to be three distinct sets made by five-toed individuals that clearly walked bipedally.

The impressions varied in depth and size, with the largest measuring fourteen to fifteen inches in length, others measuring eleven to twelve inches in length, while some were a mere eight inches. The tracks were certainly within human range, yet showed little to no evidence of an arch and appeared to be quite flat-footed with an unusually large big toe, traits consistent with suspected Bigfoot tracks.[xv] This doesn't rule out the possibility that the impressions were left by some adventurous, flat-footed hikers, of course, but none of them looked typical of human anatomy. The fact that they were small didn't rule out a Bigfoot either. These creatures would naturally be of various ages and sizes, not simply eight-foot-tall, hulking giants from birth, so the rather small size of the footprints could be attributed to juveniles.

The location itself seemed to be an unlikely place for humans to be walking around barefooted. As I mentioned, it was about a mile from the nearest road and only accessible by traipsing through an uncharted mass of rugged woods full of tangled briars, sharp sticks, pinecones, and other debris, not to mention it's home to venomous snakes, chiggers, and a variety of spiders. Perhaps hikers might remove their shoes and walk through the sandy creek barefoot, yet not one boot or shoe print was found near the barefoot tracks to suggest hikers had descended into the creek bed, removed their shoes, and then strolled around au naturel.

By the time I arrived at the creek bed, as expected, the tracks were no longer visible. The weathering that occurred over the previous weeks had wiped out all traces of them like the lines of an Etch A Sketch toy when it's shaken. The others and I searched high and low along each bend of the creek but found no new tracks. It was a disappointment, but I suppose it was lucky enough that the previous batch had been found. It seemed like

---

xv Refer to the tracks discussed in the "Marion County Monster" and "Caddo Creature" sections. They were all noted to have an unusually large big toe.

the proverbial needle in the haystack (or in this case, pine needle in the Piney Woods) as I surveyed the area. It was trees, grass, and briars for miles in every direction, where anything could have been hiding, perhaps even watching us as we searched in the creek bed until the late afternoon sun started to drop.

Photo of a track found in a dry creek bed of the Sam Houston National Forest

(Photo by Michael Mayes)

Though the trek was not as fruitful as the group hoped, anything was still possible as long as we were roaming the Piney Woods. The place we were currently exploring was located in the southern reaches, where the trees grow as tall as Alamo legends as they crowd their way to the coastline. It is part of a major hub of Texas Bigfoot activity that stretches from the national forests of Sam Houston, Angelina, and Davy Crockett to the aptly named and massive Big Thicket on down to the confluence of the Trinity, Sabine, Neches, and other significant watersheds as they flood their way into the Gulf of Mexico. Sighting reports here, like other areas of Texas, date back many years and dot the map with an ever-increasing number of pinholes. As I looked around, I was sure that if Bigfoot chose to reside in the Lone Star State, these big thickets would be yet another, very likely home.

Sam Houston Hairy Ones

The Sam Houston National Forest is comprised of 163,037 acres, intermingled with privately owned timberland and farms throughout Montgomery, San Jacinto, and Walker counties. Named in honor of the man who ultimately liberated Texas from Mexican rule, Sam Houston Forest not only offers a world of scenic beauty within the heart of Texas but also one of the highest concentrations of Bigfoot reports in the entire state.

In one of the oldest Walker County reports, a woman re-counts an incident that allegedly happened to her late husband when he was young, around 1960. While he and his friends were hanging out at a cabin near Bedias Creek one night, they saw a "six-foot-tall-plus being." The boys were familiar with a local legend that said a hermit lived in the woods, but the thing they saw didn't seem human—even by woodland hermit standards. According to her husband, it was very large, wore no clothes, and was "totally covered with long dark hair, about 4-6 inches long, all over." It also had a rank odor "like a moldy skunk."[125] He didn't specifically call it a Bigfoot, but the description undoubtedly fits the profile.

Lee Lockhart once told me of a strange encounter he had in the area of Walker County sometime in the mid-1970s. At the time, Lockhart was living near Huntsville and as an avid hunter, he spent quite a bit of time in the Sam Houston National Forest. One morning before sunlight he drove to an area known as Thickett Branch, where he planned to hunt. He parked his truck along a dirt road and proceeded to get ready. Once he had his hunting gear on, he switched on his D-cell flashlight and started walking up an old trail toward his hunting spot. Just about the time he got into the thick tree cover, something bolted from the brush and ran parallel to the trail. He swung his flashlight toward the sound and caught a glimpse of some kind of large animal covered in dark hair moving through the trees. He could not see its full body, but whatever it was stood taller than a man and appeared to be much broader and thicker. He said it was like "seeing a huge hog jump up and run," but this thing was more massive and not on four legs; it was running upright.

The hunter only saw it for a few seconds, but he felt certain it wasn't a bear by the way it ran so adeptly and how its shoulders were not sloped, but broad. Lockhart stopped walking the moment he saw the thing and kept his flashlight on it until it went out of sight in the dense brush.

Lockhart was rather shaken by the incident, so he turned and quickly walked back to his truck where he waited awhile before getting up enough courage to resume his walk to the hunting spot. He wondered if the thing had been standing there watching him the entire time he was getting ready at the truck. The thought chilled him.

At the time, he could not imagine what it could have been. Bigfoot was not something he even considered until years later. He admitted that could not be certain it was a Bigfoot, but he had never been able to explain what he saw.

Another report from the same county and general time period was submitted to the Texas Bigfoot Research Center. A young woman said that in 1975 she was paddling through the waters of Lake Raven in Huntsville State Park with her nephew when something caught her attention at the shoreline.

"It was an animal in the form of a man, all dark-haired,

blackish or dark dark-brown," she noted in her report. "It was running away from us to the left. It ran so fast with long strides."[126]

The witness was so frightened by the thing, she began to panic and started paddling furiously in the opposite direction. It happened so quickly her nephew had not seen it. Like Lockhart, to this day, she wonders just what it was she saw.

Lake Conroe, whose shores extend into the Sam Houston Forest, is another body of water that seems attractive to the creatures. In 1978, an elderly man burst into a general store near the lake saying he'd seen a "monster." The man, who was obviously shaken, told the clerk that some kind of creature had been killing hogs on his property. He said he finally got a look at it when the creature crossed the road in front of his car as he drove toward the store that morning. He tried to convince several locals in the store to follow him back to his property to investigate, but no one was willing to accompany him.[127]

Though no one stepped up, at least one patron in the store knew more then he would admit at the time. In a report fielded by former Grand Prairie police officer, David Hestand (brother of my colleague, Jerry Hestand), the patron—a man who also lived in the area—claimed that just two weeks prior he was fishing near a boat ramp along Lake Conroe when he began to hear movement in the brush about one hundred yards from the bank. The sun was starting to go down, and the area had a lot of moss hanging from the trees, so he couldn't see what it was. He figured it was just a deer until the animal started making a strange grunting/growling noise and snapping tree limbs as though it were angry. The man had hunted and fished in the area all of his life, and he knew full well this was no typical animal. The hair on the back of his neck stood on end as he began to worry. What if the thing were to rush out into the water?

The man quickly cranked up his outboard motor and sped toward the boat ramp. Once he got ashore, he hurriedly loaded the boat onto his car trailer and, in colloquial terms, "got the hell out of there." He admittedly never laid eyes on the animal but felt it could have been the very same creature seen by the man who burst into the store.

During a personal interview with the Hestand brothers, the man pointed out the location on a map. The Hestands were stunned. They had previously interviewed a witness who said that on August 16, 2003, he fired a gun at what he described as an eight-foot-tall, four-hundred-pound, hairy, human-like thing that was standing in his backyard adjacent to the national forest.[128] Though twenty-five years apart, the locations of the sightings were virtually identical. Could it be mere coincidence?[xvi]

In a case investigated by members of the North American Wood Ape Conservancy, a man said he saw what looked like a Bigfoot east of Lake Conroe in 2001. The witness said he was driving along FM 1375 at 5:30 a.m. headed to work. Just after he crossed the bridge heading east, he pulled over to relieve himself because he'd been drinking too much coffee. There was a spot where fishermen had worn a path from the road to the lake, so he walked a few feet down to do his business. As he did, he smelled a "really strange skunk odor" followed by a distinct "woofing noise." The hair on the back of his neck stood up, and when he turned his head in the direction of the noise, he saw something stand up.[129]

"I had left my lights on in the truck and though they were not shining in my direction, the reflection was enough," he reported. "It stood well over a foot taller than me and was still below me on the slope of the embankment."

He went on to describe the figure as being approximately seven feet tall with dark-colored hair and a large head. It also had long arms and reeked of the horrible musky odor. "It began to make a squealing bark kind of noise and in two or three strides

---

xvi For more details about this case, refer to the book *Hunting Apes in America* by Jerry Hestand.

was past me and headed for the road," he continued. "I don't know why it didn't turn and head back into the forest but it didn't."

As the thing crossed the road, a truck came around the curve and braked, presumably having seen the creature as well. The creature then walked up a hill on the other side of the road and disappeared into the trees. The witness got back into his truck and raced away.

In January 2016, NAWAC received another report from the very same road. The witness said he was driving near the bridge one morning at around 5:00 a.m. when he noticed eyes reflecting in the headlights. He first thought it was a deer, but as he got closer he could see the distinct shape of something standing upright on two legs. It was huge, much larger than a person, and perhaps as tall as eight feet. Startled, the witness swerved to the opposite lane as the thing watched him. He was certain it wasn't a human . . . not even one in a costume.[130]

A man claimed to have seen a strange creature in the neighboring county of San Jacinto in 1983. According to the report, the man was scouting for deer signs when he and his fellow hunters saw an unidentified creature run out of the woods and cross a clearing.

"It looked a lot like a monkey, in a way, but it ran on two legs, and never once to my knowledge did it ever use its hands to assist in its motion of travel," he stated. "It was black in color, approximately four [feet] tall, and was really fast."[131]

Canadian Bigfoot researcher John Green also has reports from the area in his extensive files. In a letter dated December 28, 1992, an individual recounted an incident from 1981 in which a woman by the name of Dee Hayes was driving to work through the Sam Houston National Forest at approximately 5:30 a.m. As she rounded a curve in the road, she could see a seven-to-eight-foot-tall, brown animal standing on two legs near the side of the road fifty yards away. She stopped and watched the creature until it turned and entered the timber. She described it as having a "gorilla-like head with no noticeable snout."[132]

In November 1997, a woman had a startling daytime sighting while driving through the forest southeast of Waverly. It was around 11:00 a.m. and she was driving one of her daughter's friends home. The two girls were in the back seat, talking and laughing, while the woman navigated along the curvy road near their home. As she rounded a bend, she noticed what she thought was a horse standing in the thicket.

"I am facing the road and looking into the thicket ahead, and 60 to 80 feet from my car I see what I first thought was the haunches of a horse moving around," she explained. "I could only see the top part. What I saw had shiny reddish hair and was like 7 to 8 feet high."[133]

The road was not in the best condition with a deep runoff on one side and various downed limbs littered about, so she had to keep her speed below fifteen miles per hour. As she continued toward the animal, it became apparent it wasn't a horse.

"As I go up this curve toward this thing, I start to look at it closer," she continued. "Then this thing . . . turns around and looks straight at me then crouches down and tries to hide behind a little tree and it's sitting there looking at me. I drove within 15 to 20 feet of it, as I drove by I turned my head and looked out the window."

Whatever it was had "big, thick arms and legs" and had a look of surprise on its face, as if it were just as surprised to see the car as the witness was to see it. The woman was so frightened she did not stop. She was afraid the thing might spring up and come toward her slow-moving car. A short distance further she asked the girls in the back if they had seen it. They said they did not since they were busy talking to each other. The mother figured that was for the best. She was startled enough.

"After that I didn't go into the woods anymore," she confessed. "We had 2 ½ acres, we had cleared about 1 acre of our land and I wanted to clear all of it. I didn't like the woods that close to the house, I wanted to see what was out there. I started closing the curtains at night, put lights all around the house. When I drove home I would turn on the high beams to make sure there was nothing out there on our property."

She was not the only witness to be frightened in the county. In 2009, just a short distance east of her property, a photographer for *Texas Highways* magazine was hiking around getting some nature shots when he heard some loud crashing in the thicket on the other side of a clearing. Before he could react, a small juvenile black bear darted from the brush, stopped at the edge of the clearing, and began sniffing the air. The photographer started to pursue it for a photo opportunity but thought the better of it since the mother might have been nearby. He decided at that point to walk back the way he'd come to give the animals some space.

"I had barely turned when I saw a huge, dark shape about ten to twelve feet away through some very thick yaupon brush," he said in his report. "I'm 6'3" and I was looking up at a twenty to thirty degree angle to its head and huge shoulders."[134]

The photographer knew that bears in Texas don't get anywhere near that size, so he was perplexed as to what kind of animal it was. "All of a sudden its hand moved and a 2–3" diameter tree trunk about fifteen feet long came flying toward me," he said.

The man turned and ran, fearing for his life. Once he reached his car, he jumped in and drove away from the area as fast as he could. It was an experience he could have never imagined. "I parked the car and sat there until quite late as I pondered what had happened. It was only then that I concluded I might have just encountered a Sasquatch."

In 2007, an uncanny series of events in Montgomery County further supported the notion that an unknown bipedal entity stalks the woods of the Sam Houston Forest. The first incident occurred on the morning of September 19. At approximately 2:00 a.m., a construction employee working on a new sports facility in The Woodlands was taking a cigarette break when he noticed an upright, bipedal figure step from the woods surrounding the complex. He described it as exceptionally tall and covered in dark hair. The figure was only visible a few seconds before it slipped back into the trees.[135]

A few days later, on September 21, two security officers were patrolling the same construction area at 2:20 a.m. when they spotted a huge, bipedal figure walking near the construction office trailers where some makeshift lights had been placed. As they watched the figure from a distance of approximately thirty yards, they could see it stood at least seven feet tall and appeared to be covered in dark hair. It also walked with an unusually long stride, powerful gait, and a slight "slump," all of which did not look human.[136]

After the thing moved out of sight, the officers reluctantly placed a call to 911, as per company policy whenever a trespasser was seen, regardless of its appearance. Police were dispatched—no doubt believing it was probably a human—but no further signs of the trespasser were found. In an interview with NAWAC investigators, the security officer that made the 911 call remained adamant that what he and his partner saw was not a person. He also claimed to have no knowledge of the previous sighting prior to his call.

Five weeks later, a woman reported a similar encounter just one mile from the construction facility. As she and her husband were driving one afternoon, they noticed a "hunched brown figure walking through the trees."[137] As in the other cases, it appeared to be tall, hairy, and human-like. Had the new construction in The Woodlands uprooted an unknown resident? Given the corroborating reports, it's certainly possible.

Stories of Bigfoot continue to ebb out in a slow, steady

flow from the areas surrounding the forest. In some cases the creatures have been said to even be aggressive, attacking unsuspecting campers and causing them to flee for their lives, or worse. These tales of a more deadly, sensational nature have yet to be substantiated, but there's no doubt that seeing one of these things would be life-changing at the very least. And if it were to begin walking toward you or act aggressively, it would be all the more frightening.

Imagine for a moment if you came face to face with a huge, hulking, ape-like figure in the middle of the woods. A creature as large and muscular as a gorilla, yet it stands fully upright, towering above. As it looks down, its eyes are dark and penetrating yet so human-like that it hints at an intelligence far beyond that of any other animal known to this world. It's an encounter no one could ever quite prepare for.

Entering the Sam Houston National Forest
(Photo by Chris Buntenbah)

Caught on Film?

On November 3, 1997, the nationally syndicated television show *Strange Universe* kicked off its daily episode with the words "Captured On Video" splashed across the screen. The show's host, Emmett Miller, appeared shortly thereafter to announce that Bigfoot had been filmed in a most unlikely place. "Settle back," he said, "for real-life close encounters of the strange kind, beginning with the *Texas Bigfoot*."[138]

The show then aired a never-before-seen video of what appears to be a tall, hair-covered creature running in a somewhat zig-zag fashion through some tall pines. The subject is perhaps thirty yards from the camera, partially obscured by the trees and foliage as it moves along. The film is low-resolution tape quality but clear enough to see that whatever the thing is, it's definitely anthropomorphic and upright on two legs.

The footage was submitted to *Strange Universe* by a Texas gunsmith named Danny Sweeten, who comments on it during the course of the show. His story details are sporadic amid the quick cuts; however, the full story would later be documented as various researchers and radio shows interviewed Sweeten at length.[xvii]

According to Sweeten, he filmed the creature two years prior on October 5, 1995. That day he had gone to a rural area near Cleveland, Texas, about forty miles north of Houston, to look at some property he and a friend were thinking about purchasing in order to open a gun range. The friend had loaned Sweeten a VHS video camcorder so he could film the land to view later since he was unable to accompany him.

Sweeten said when he reached the property (located near the Sam Houston National Forest), he began filming as he walked along the property line. Suddenly, he came upon a creature that

---

xvii As of this writing, the footage can be viewed on YouTube. Search "Texas Bigfoot Danny Sweeten" or go to this link: https://youtu.be/scfQZJGPHRs

was stretched out on the ground with its head resting on its elbow, as if it were "laying there like it had just got up from a nap."[139]

When the thing saw Sweeten, it got up and ran toward him as if it were angry. In seconds, it hit Sweeten in the chest and sent him flying backward. Sweeten flipped over and landed face-down. The impact was so hard he said it knocked two of his teeth loose. The creature then retreated and started running away through the trees. The gunsmith said he quickly grabbed the camera and began filming. The camera did not have a rubber eyepiece so rather than put the viewfinder up to his eye to aim, he held the camera out "like a rifle" and shot the footage as best he could.

Sweeten said he was so scared by the encounter that once the creature was out of sight, he got up and ran out of the woods as fast as he could. He had a gun with him, but it was unloaded, so he couldn't use it during the frenzy.

Once Sweeten returned home, he shared the story and the footage with a few friends before ultimately deciding to shelve it. He was so worried that people would ridicule him, he thought it would be best to just keep the story quiet.

That's how the situation remained for nearly two years until, according to Sweeten, he began to be harassed by a man named "Kevin Tolbert" who said he worked for the "Federal Wildlife Protection Agency." (There is no such agency.) Tolbert allegedly told Sweeten to turn over the tape. Sweeten refused, although he was growing tired of Tolbert's constant harassment. Finally, Sweeten reached out to the *Strange Universe* television show and arranged to sell them the rights. He figured no one could bother him if he no longer owned the footage, not to mention he could use the money from the sale to fix his loose teeth.

When the video aired, the response by viewers and Bigfoot researchers was split. Some researchers, like renowned cryptozoologist, Loren Coleman, and founder of the Texas Bigfoot Research Center, Craig Woolheater, felt it might actually depict an authentic creature. Others, such as famed Yeti hunter Peter Byrne, felt it "looked like a man in a fur suit."[140]

Sweeten himself, who stood behind the authenticity of his film, described the creature in more detail during later interviews. In a conversation with Tennessee Bigfoot researcher, Scott McNabb, Sweeten explained the creature had "a crest at the back of the head that angled to a sloping forehead, and it appeared as if the face had been lowered down. The eyes were gray and had a human shape but sat wider apart than human eyes do. The nose was not flat like a gorilla, but a mix between a Caucasian nose and an African American nose. Hair covered the face except the eyes, nose, and mouth, and was in a fashion like a man with a full facial beard. Skin color on the face was a grayish/whitish looking color. The creature's body was large and bulky with a V-shaped torso and a protruding gut area. The hair was brown/black, the body was a brownish color, and the tops of the hands were black. The hair appeared to be very coarse, like a wild hog's hair."[141]

Artist rendering of the subject in Sweeten's video

(Illustration by Ashley Cheree)

Sweeten went on to describe many other specific details, which either points to the fact that he actually saw one of these things or that he has a great imagination. McNabb, who interviewed him at length and pressed on various inconsistencies noted in Sweeten's retellings of the event, believed his credibility was severely lacking. Sweeten had also appeared on the popular syndicated radio show, *Coast To Coast AM*, where he shared the story with host Art Bell, so there were different tellings of the story to compare.

As the footage and the story made the rounds, the now infamous Texas Bigfoot film continued to garner controversy. The late Dr. Grover Krantz, an anthropologist who was a strong proponent for the existence of Bigfoot, analyzed the footage and found issues. Krantz pointed out that the subject in Sweeten's film walked with "locked knees." Locked knees is a human locomotion trait while most researchers believe Sasquatch would walk in a bent-knee fashion. Krantz also noted that the subject appears to be rather tall and thin, devoid of the biomechanics, skeletal structure, or muscle tone that would surely be present in an authentic creature of this type.

Issues with the actual footage aside, many continued to question Sweeten's credibility, especially when he came forward with supposed new footage and an audio recording. The audio was quickly identified as having been created with a deer call, possibly blown through a tube to give it a more depth. The video footage showed another alleged Bigfoot stepping from the woods into view of the camera. The camera initially pans back and forth several times before finally stopping on a spot where the subject walks into frame. McNabb obtained a copy of the new footage and sent it to video analysis expert Dave Bittner. Bittner noted that:

> *The video is shot very wide, which hides any details of the subject. At one point, the shooter zooms in slightly, then stops. Why didn't the shooter zoom in more?*

It is very difficult to form any solid conclusions based on the video footage provided, for a variety of reasons, but there are several aspects which lead me to question its authenticity. When the video starts, the shooter spends several seconds panning back and forth around the area where the alleged Bigfoot appears. On more than one occasion, the shooter seems to hesitate around the area where the subject later appears. This could merely be a coincidence, or it could be that the shooter was expecting the subject's appearance.[142]

Given the suspicious nature of both films and the wild story provided by Sweeten, it's hard to know whether any of the material is legitimate. Either way, the original footage remains a controversial piece of Texas Bigfoot history and one that despite itself, helped to raise awareness that such creatures may not be exclusive to the Pacific Northwest.

Angelina Ape Files

Back in October 1972, the Texas Parks and Wildlife Department received a curious call from a professor at Stephen F. Austin State University. Apparently four of his students had encountered a very unusual animal while camping in the Angelina National Forest. Normally the rangers wouldn't respond in person to such a call, but in this case the professor sounded on the level. And it wasn't the first time the department had received reports of a peculiar creature said to inhabit that area.[143]

A ranger was dispatched to location, which was a camp about five miles down a logging road, deep in the heart of the Angelina forest. When the officer arrived at the camp, he met with the professor and ten students who were part of the group. They told him of the situation with a mix of excitement and concern.

The four students said they were the last of the group sitting around the campfire at about 2:00 a.m. the night before, when they heard something circling the camp. It sounded big and heavy as its footsteps crunched through the woods. They had a Coleman lantern burning in addition to the fire, but the woods beyond the flickering lights were too shadowed to see whatever it was.

After listening to the sound for a while, the students decided to check it out. They grabbed their flashlights and carefully walked into the woods. As the beams of the battery-lights pierced the darkness, they noticed movement behind a tree. All four shined their light in that direction. A bizarre animal stepped into the hazy yellow beams.

The boys were taken aback. The "animal" was standing on two legs at a height of about five feet. It was covered in light-colored hair and had a stocky build. They estimated its weight was about two hundred and fifty pounds. The thing just stood there looking at them for about five second before it suddenly jumped, from a standing position, over a very wide ditch. It then ran into the darkness of the woods.

The boys were frightened and immediately fled back to the campsite and woke up the rest of the group. When they explained what they had seen, the professor felt certain they were not playing a joke. The boys were clearly upset, and they had all gotten a good look at the thing.

The following morning the students searched the area where they had seen the animal and found strange footprints that appeared to have three toes and a nub for a fourth. The evidence seemed to support their claim; one that was by all accounts legitimate, but that could not easily be explained.

Suffice to say, the Angelina National Forest is yet another heavily timbered segment of the southern Texas thickets where again we find reports of curious ape-like creatures going back many years. Four years before the students encountered their creature, a couple was parked in a wooded area of Angelina County east of Peavy Switch when they suddenly got the feeling they were being watched. They looked out the driver's side window and saw a huge, man-like thing looking at them from about six feet away. It was tall, dark, and clearly visible in the light of the full moon as it bent down to look into the window. The overhead lighting gave it a silhouette-like appearance against the sandy roadbed.

"I turned around to look at my girlfriend, and when her eyes met mine, she started screaming in a panic," the witness told my late colleague, Charles DeVore. "The 'creature' had a rounded head, which sloped down to its shoulders—as if it had no neck. Its eyes were large and almond-shaped [and] the shoulders were extremely wide."[144]

The witness started the car and quickly sped away. He dropped his panicked girlfriend off at her parents and rounded up some friends so he could go back to investigate. He was still trying to get his head around what they had seen. By the time they made it back to the location, however, there was no sign of the creature. They sat in the darkness for quite some time listening to strange howls and dogs barking, but still the unknown creature did not return.

Where there's one report, there's usually another. Sure enough, two men claimed to have seen a creature outside of Peavy Switch one night in 1979 while hunting rabbits. When they came upon it in the car, it was squatting down beside the road. It gave off an intense, rotten smell.

"When my friend shined his light into its eyes it stood, snorted and turned back into the clear-cut," Charles V. said.[145] Needless to say, he floored it and sped from the area. He'd heard stories about such things all his life, but until that moment did not consider the possibility of Bigfoot in Texas.

The possibility of Bigfoot in Texas has not been a question for Bobby Hamilton, a Texan who has become one of the most notable figures in the search for Southern Bigfoot. Hamilton has spent much of his adult life trying to solve the mystery, and in 1997, he founded the Gulf Coast Bigfoot Research Organization. Like the Texas Bigfoot Research Center, the GCBRO has been an important resource for information, as it has not only collected and published various encounter reports, but also organized numerous searches for the alleged beasts. Hamilton has reported several personal encounters over the years, but the one that initially set him on the journey was a rather disturbing incident he experienced as a child. In one of our conversations, Hamilton told me of that fateful night when Bigfoot transformed from legend to life in the worst way possible.

It was 1969, and the Hamiltons were living in Nacogdoches County, deep in the thickets north of the Angelina National Forest and not far from the Sabine River Bottoms. His father worked in the offshore pipeline business, so he would be gone for extended periods. During those times, Bobby and his two older brothers would often sleep in their mother's room on makeshift pallets.[xviii]

One night Bobby, who was just shy of five years old, had to get up to use the bathroom. He felt scared so he woke up his older brother, Gerald, and asked if he would go to the bathroom with him.

"I don't know why I woke up scared, but I kept begging him to walk me to the bathroom," Hamilton explained. "I don't know if I was scared because I sensed something or what. We lived in an old farmhouse, and there was a lot of weird stuff going on around the house, though we didn't know what it was at the time."

Gerald refused to get up, but assured Bobby that it was okay and that he would stay awake until he got back. Bobby finally stopped pleading and scurried down the hall to the bathroom. Everything was fine until he returned to his mother's room.

---

xviii A *pallet* is a common Southern term meaning a makeshift bed on the floor made out of a stack of blankets or other materials.

There were two windows with screens in the room, both of them open slightly to let in as much breeze as possible. It was warm and they didn't have air conditioning, so the windows usually remained open at night with the curtains pulled back.

"As I came walking back I got about two steps into the door [of the bedroom] when I heard something scratch the screen," Hamilton explained. "When I looked up, I could see the teeth of this thing and a hand motion like it was motioning for me to come to it."

The night was bright with moonlight, providing enough illumination to see thing outside. Young Bobby froze in terror as it beckoned him to the window. It was some kind of creature unlike anything he was familiar with.

"I froze for a second and the next thing I know, I dove to my left and landed on my other brother who was about seven years older than me and started choking him and was screaming," Hamilton recalled. "He woke up and threw me off and looked up to see this thing turn from the window. He didn't get a real good look at it; he just saw something turn and run."

By now everyone was awake and scrambling to figure out what was going on. Once Bobby had calmed down and told them what he had seen, his older brothers grabbed their rifles and flashlights and hurried outside to investigate. They could see where something had scuffed the dirt under the window while it was standing there, but they did not see the creature—or whatever it was.

His older brother Gerald did not see the creature that night, but years later confirmed that he, too, had seen the thing on three occasions. Each time he had been awakened from sleep to find the creature looking in his bedroom window.

"This thing would be at the window motioning for him to come to the window," Hamilton told me. "It would be motioning and showing its teeth like he was grinning." Gerald, too, was so shaken he didn't even want to talk about it. He kept the details of his sighting to himself for many years before sharing with Bobby.

The Hamiltons eventually moved from the house, but Bobby never forgot the events of the night and vowed to find out just what kind of creature it was that scared him and his brothers so badly. It was a rather traumatizing spark that ignited a lifelong investigation that has taken him to wooded regions all across Texas and Louisiana. In addition to his work as director of the Gulf Coast Bigfoot Research Organization, Hamilton was also a cast member on the rather controversial television series *Killing Bigfoot* that aired on the *Destination America* channel from 2016 to 2020. So far no Bigfoots have been harmed in the making of this show, but the intent to bring in a specimen in order to prove these things do exist has continued to be a focus of Hamilton's efforts.

In one of my own investigations I spoke to Steven Woodson, who told me of an experience he had in December 1991 while hunting in the thickets of Angelina County. At the time he was with his brother, Jim, and a mutual friend. They were walking along an old logging trail at about 3:30 p.m. when they stopped for a bathroom break. Just as they were picking up their guns to resume the hike, the three men saw a large, hair-covered animal run across the trail approximately fifteen feet in front of them. It was running on two legs and was visible for a few seconds before heading into the woods on the other side of the trail.

"It was covered in gray hair and looked very muscular," Woodson told me. He estimated its height at around seven to eight feet and weight at around five hundred pounds. He described it as having a conical-shaped head, similar to a gorilla, and even compared its muscular form to that of a silverback. However, he said its legs were definitely longer as it ran upright much like a human.

After the creature ran into the timber, they could see the top of a large tree swaying back and forth as though the animal was pushing it. The men followed it into the woods to get a better look, but after a short distance they decided it might be best to leave the creature alone.

The following year, Steve's brother, Jim, encountered a similar creature in the same area. He told me he was hunting along a steep levee embankment of the Neches River at the time. As he climbed up the levee, he set his gun on higher ground so he could get better traction. At the point where his head reached the top of the levee, just enough to see the level ground beyond, he was startled by the sight of a hairy, bipedal creature walking just a few feet away. The creature turned and looked directly at him, although it kept walking, seemingly indifferent to the human presence. Frightened (and now without a gun), Jim ducked down and remained on the side of the embankment where he watched the creature for another twenty seconds until it was out of sight. Jim then scrambled to the top, grabbed his rifle, and high-tailed it out of the woods.

An abandoned home on the outskirts of the Angelina Forest
(Photo by Lyle Blackburn)

In our discussions, both Steve and Jim recalled a vague warning their uncle had issued when they were younger. He wasn't specific but was unusually stern when he told them to be careful in those particular woods. Now they knew just what he meant.

Marauding Monkeymen

People living in the area of Dayton, Texas, have long reported an ape-like creature in their area. Known locally as the "Dayton Monkeyman" or "Monkeyman of 1409," this creature is yet another Bigfoot candidate said to inhabit the swamps and tangled thickets of coastal Texas at the tail end of the Trinity River.

Reports of the creature date back to at least the 1950s, and nearly every witness who reports an encounter with the alleged beast notes that they've often heard tales of it previously by way of their parents or grandparents. Some report it as a tall, ape-like creature while others describe it as being somewhat smaller, much like a "large monkey" that has the ability to run on two legs.

In his book, *In the Big Thicket: On the Trail of the Wild Man*, my late friend and Big Thicket expert, Rob Riggs, recounts an alleged sighting told to him by a witness. The young man said he was at his home near Dayton one night when he heard a disturbance outside in his rabbit pens. When he went out to investigate, he saw a "large, dark form" in the moonlight as it fled into the woods with one of his rabbits. The witness impulsively chased the mysterious thief, following the squeals of its hapless prey. Upon reaching the river bank a short distance away, he watched "as what looked like a huge ape-like animal swam to the other side of the river, easily negotiating the strong current, and never letting go of the rabbit."[146]

In the winter of 1993, a man was squirrel hunting near Dayton when he came face to face with the thing. In his own words:

> *I was squirrel hunting on my grandmother's property that is around 2-1/2 miles east of Dayton. I had just walked in a clearing, surrounded by dense foliage. I was looking up into the trees for any sign of squirrels when I caught a movement out of the corner of my right eye. I looked down and to the front of me and saw, standing about 15 feet away, a very large creature. It was about 6 feet to 7 feet tall, very broad shouldered, and very hairy except the face. The face was devoid of hair. Coal black eyes, wide nose, very long arms and big hands. It was like I had surprised it. We stared at each other for about 10 seconds, when I cocked my 12 gauge [shotgun]. At that time it turned to its right and disappeared. VERY quickly. It was getting to be dusk but I did look for tracks and found none. There was no smell.*
>
> *I hunted at that location quite often and know the surroundings. That day there were no birds, squirrels or any signs of wildlife whatsoever. It started to get darker so I started home.*
>
> *Each person has their own account of these encounters, which include sightings, unusually large footprints in nearby creek bottom, strong smells, unidentifiable sounds, and uncomfortable feelings of being watched and stalked. It makes the hair stand up on the back of your neck. These incidents date back to the early 1950s.*[147]

On July 14, 2003, the editors of a dining blog for Liberty County received the following unexpected email:

> *According to some people who live on 1409 in Dayton, and confirmed by at least one county deputy, off duty,*

people who live in that area have been calling in to the law officers and reporting that they have sighted a short creature scurrying around their neighborhoods that has been nicknamed the "monkey man" due to its appearance. I was just wondering if anyone that uses this site has seen it or knows anything about it?[148]

The editors were skeptical, so they contacted the Liberty County Sheriff's Department for verification. To their surprise, the office confirmed that they had indeed taken reports of what they called the "Monkey Man of 1409." As a result they had increased patrols, primarily in the area of County Road 450, but so far none of the deputies had actually seen it.

An email was sent the following day to Texas Bigfoot Research Center, alerting them to the situation. The writer included details about one of the sightings saying that a "four-foot, muscular monkey man had been seen on a resident's roof as he pulled into his driveway."[149] The resident said it leaped off the house and ran into the woods. The witness in this case was reluctant to share the story himself because he had already been ridiculed quite a bit when he informed his neighbors.

While this incident remains unverified, other incidents continued to be reported. On January 2, 2004, a couple was driving toward the Trinity River Bridge in Liberty County after midnight when the male (driver) noticed something in the center of the road. His girlfriend was dozing off, so he yelled to alert her that they might have an accident if he couldn't stop their truck in time.

"She sat up and screamed that we were about to hit "him,'" the man reported. "I locked the brakes of her truck up and when I did whatever it was stood up in the road and started to run to our right towards the woods."[150]

The truck came to stop and at that point they could see there was a dead deer in the center of the road. Whatever it was had been apparently inspecting or feeding on the carcass.

"My girlfriend started to open her door and I grabbed her to stop her," the man continued. "She yelled that it was a 'Bigfoot'. By the time I looked up from her, the creature was standing on the side of the road watching us. When she opened her door the creature made like a squalling sound and turned into the woods."

When interviewed by Daryl Colyer of the Texas Bigfoot Research Center, the female was quite concerned that if her story got out, people would think she was "nuts." She and her boyfriend had already told her mother, who scoffed and tried to convince them it was a coyote. But both witnesses knew better. Coyotes don't stand up and walk off on two legs.

Stories of "monkeymen" are not exclusive to Dayton. In the summer of 2004, the *El Campo Leader-News* reported that residents had been calling the Matagorda County Sheriff's Office to report sightings of a similar animal that looked like "an overgrown monkey." In one instance, a woman and her husband saw it near their rural home. The husband tried to shoot it with a pistol, but it ran off too quickly.[151]

Police were summoned to the home where the couple told them the creature was "grayish and had a man-like face, but its nose was flatter than a human nose." They said it was around five feet tall.

In 2019, a resident in Santa Fe, Texas (sixty miles south of Dayton near the Gulf Coast) reported something nearly identical. According to *The Independent*, the alarm was raised in the early hours of September 9, when a woman named Patricia de la Mora called police to report she had seen "some kind of primate causing pandemonium" near her home. She said she was sleeping when she was awakened by a loud crash of thunder. It was followed by some "strange noises" outside her home, so she eventually got up and opened the curtains to look out. When she did, she saw something resembling a "big monkey" in the street. By the time police arrived, however, the thing was gone.[152]

The following day, police received yet another hair-raising call. This time it was from a woman who said a big "monkey" tried to attack her while she was checking her mail. She claimed she spent twenty minutes hiding in her car until it ran off.

The creature was later accused of trying to snatch a cat and even grab a child, but police could never substantiate the claims.

This doesn't sound much like Bigfoot, but even if it was some sort of known primate, the authorities seemed to have had little luck in catching up with it. The witnesses were earnest in their statements, yet nothing could be found. Perhaps it's not as easy as one would think to find a rogue creature running amok . . . even under the watchful eyes of a city. In the miles of endless thickets, it would surely be far more difficult . . . perhaps nearly impossible.

Ol' Mossyback

The last stop on this Texas-sized search is in the deepest heart of the Piney Woods, a place known as the Big Thicket. It's a massive, loosely defined area that occupies all or part of at least six counties and includes areas between the Neches River on the east, the Trinity River on the west, Pine Island Bayou on the south, to the higher Eocene geological formations to the north. As the bold name suggests, this is a land full of dense woods, thick brush, snaking creeks, and blackwater bogs that is often impenetrable. It's also a place of vast biological diversity caused by ice age glaciers that pushed the contrasting ecosystems of hardwood forests, prairies, coastal plains, and swamps into one compact area. For this reason, it is often referred to as "the biological crossroads of America."[153]

The Big Thicket is so rugged, outlaws were said to have used it as a hideout, since only the hardiest of lawmen would dare challenge the terrain filled with alligators, snakes, wildcats, and bears. Perhaps not surprisingly, the Big Thicket is also home to a healthy helping of strangeness including reports of spook lights, ghostly Native warriors, and assorted Bigfoot creatures.

According to Big Thicket expert Rob Riggs: "For years people in the area between the Thicket's western edge along the Pine Island Bayou and the Trinity River swamp had occasionally caught glimpses of something large, hairy and not quite human," a creature the locals call "Ol' Mossyback."[154]

In his book, *In the Big Thicket: On the Trail of the Wild Man*, Riggs recounts statements from several young men who claimed multiple sightings of an ape-like creature in the Big Thicket National Preserve close to the small town of Saratoga. The boys spent much of their spare time hiking through the Thicket—since there was little else to do—and were therefore very familiar with the local wildlife. This creature, they assured him, was definitely something out of the ordinary.

The first time they saw it, the animal was running on all fours across a rice field. They were in a truck at a distance of several hundred yards, so very little detail could be observed beyond the fact it looked ape-like. The next time they saw the creature, or one like it, it was creeping around an old bridge at dusk. This time they were much closer and could see that it walked in a bipedal fashion. The third encounter occurred near a sludge pit, which had been part of an old oil field installation. In this instance they saw what they believed was the same animal right around dusk. As they watched, it let out a long howl before slipping into the woods, never to be seen again.

The multiple encounters seem almost "too lucky," but Riggs heard similar stories from a woman in the area who claimed her family had also seen an ape-like creature on several occasions. One time they saw it near a sludge pit. By all accounts this woman and the boys did not know each other.

Sightings on record go back to at least the 1950s and have continued until the present day. A witness reported that in 1964, he was visiting a rural cemetery in Polk County with a friend and his mother when they heard something crashing through the woods at the rear of the grounds. They looked over and saw a "large, dark, hairy creature" standing behind the back fence approximately fifty yards away. The woman screamed and told the kids to get in the car. The creature turned and "shuffled back into the woods."[155]

Polk County is also the location of one of the more eerie encounters I've run across. It was November 12, 1999, and a hunter had taken his wife and four-year-old son to his hunting lease for the weekend. That morning, the man was out hunting while his wife and son remained in the camp. She was starting to prepare lunch when her son asked if "his new friend" could eat with them. Figuring it was some kind of small animal or perhaps a figment of his imagination, the woman said "sure" to humor the younger.

"When he stared to yell for his friend to stay I happened to glance up to see a very tall, hairy animal run into the woods," she told an investigator from the Gulf Coast Bigfoot Research Organization. "[It] was about 7–8 feet tall and [had a] dark and light brown mixture of hair. That was enough of a look that I took my son to the truck to sit and wait for my husband. When he arrived I made him take us home and haven't been back with him since. My son still, to this day, says that mommy ran off his 'monkey friend' and still remembers the look on the animal's face. I try to tell him it was a bear or something, but he is determined it was his monkey friend."[156]

Another woman got the shock of her life when she saw a similar animal in 2001. The woman told my colleague Monica Rawlins that she was not a "believer in Bigfoot" prior to the event, but since then her perspective had completely changed.

The woman said that it was early fall and she was cooking dinner at her home in Tyler County in the early evening. She happened to look out the kitchen window into the backyard and saw a large animal standing on two legs.

"He stood about 7–8 foot tall," she said. "It was black and hairy all over. He had arms like an ape [and] looked prehistoric."[157]

The animal was standing in profile, slightly hunched over and not moving. She had a clear view of it from approximately fifty feet. The woman watched it for a few minutes, not sure what do to. It was so surreal, she finally sat down a moment to collect her thoughts. When she returned to the window, the animal was gone. The house backed up to acres of woods that were part of the encompassing Big Thicket area, so she presumed it walked back into the trees.

Realizing she had just witnessed what was most likely a Bigfoot, she went to find her husband and son. When she told them what she had seen, her husband laughed it off, but her son decided to grab a gun and go outside to investigate. He found no signs of the creature, but after a few minutes he heard gunshots coming from the woods. This was followed by two men yelling at each other. One said "What was that?" while the other answered, "Let's get the hell out of here!"

Following the incident, the family began to speculate about other strange things that had occurred several months before. On one occasion, they were feeding their goats behind the house when they heard a "low growl" behind them. The growl was close, but it was dark and they could not see whatever was making the sound. Later, several of their young goats went missing, while others were found dead and dismembered. On other occasions, they had heard similar grunts and growls just outside the window of their home.

As they told their story to neighbors and friends, the family learned that one of them, an ambulance driver, had seen a very large animal run across the road in front of her. Another friend said her grandson had seen an ape-like animal step into a road. By all accounts, there was something unexplainable living in their woods.

A computer systems engineer named James Hendrix told me of another sighting. In the fall of 2003, he and his wife, Carrie, were driving near the Big Sandy Creek unit of the Big Thicket National Preserve in Polk County just after sundown when Hendrix caught sight of something running toward the road through his driver-side window. He immediately braked as he saw a bipedal figure leap a drainage ditch and run across the road in full view of the headlights. According to Hendrix, it ran fluidly with a bent-over posture, as if it had switched to all fours once it hit the pavement. He noted that its long arms touched the ground, but only a few times. It was about five feet tall and covered in long, reddish-brown hair.

Interpretation of the creature seen by James and Carrie Hendrix

(Illustration by Cole Carter)

"It had a very broad build and looked somewhat like an orangutan except that it had a flat face and was proportioned more like a human with long arms," Hendrix told me. The creature paused when it reached the other side of the road. It looked back at the car before entering the dark woods.

Since the creature assumed a quadrupedal stance, a bear could be considered in this case. However, Hendrix feels strongly it wasn't a bear. "It was running on two legs faster than a person before it went to all fours," he explained. His wife, Carrie, also got a good look at the face from approximately twenty feet away as it turned to look at the car. She was sure it did not have the snout of a bear.

An almost identical incident took place in November 1972, only a few miles from where Hendrix saw the strange creature. According to Donna Gilchriest Grundy, who was twelve years old at the time, she was riding in the car with her grandmother and great aunt one afternoon around 3:30 p.m. as they traveled along the Segno Fire Lane in a heavily wooded area of the Big Thicket. The road was unpaved (as it still is today) so they were driving at a slow speed. Donna was leaning forward from the back seat talking to her grandmother and great aunt, when all three saw a large, hairy, upright creature emerge from the woods and dart across the road on two legs. It missed the bumper by a mere three feet!

"It never looked at us, but we could see the body very well," Grundy told me, as we discussed the incident. "It was covered in thick, long, shaggy hair that kind of shook on its body as it ran. It had long arms and a chest that was really thick."

The trio watched as it leaped over a drainage ditch at the side of the road and quickly disappeared into the dense thicket. The creature ran in a slightly hunched-over fashion, swinging its arms as it went, and it stayed on two legs the entire time. Grundy estimated its height to be seven to eight feet tall.

"We were stunned and shocked and pretty much afraid

because we didn't know what we had just seen," she admitted. To her best recollection, she had never heard anyone talk about Bigfoot in that part of Texas at the time. It was only a year later that it seemed to make any sense.

"I remember the [Legend of] Boggy Creek movie came to Livingston [Texas] right after that and I wanted to go see it," she recalled. "And that pretty much confirmed what we saw."

Over the years, a number of people have reported hearing strange, unidentified howls coming from the darkest parts of the Thicket. It's a spooky sensation as the sounds echo across the black bogs, because you know something is out there, but you can't see it.

I received a recording of one such spooky howl from a U.S. Air Force Veteran who has spent much of his life hunting the Big Thicket in Polk County. Darryl Jones said he was sitting in a tree stand on March 25, 2017, at about 4:00 p.m. when a strange sound rose up among the trees. It was a long, howling moan that could only have come from a large animal. It was something he had never heard in all his years of hunting. Shortly after the howl rang out, the nervous howls of a wolf or coyote joined in. The strange vocal, however, was uniquely different than those of the canid.

Jones had the wherewithal to record the sound with his iPhone as it continued for several minutes. After receiving the recording, I forwarded it to an audio analysis expert who has experience in identifying unique animal sounds. "Upon review it appears that when we clear out the wolf, coyote, or dog howls there is a possible hit on two different, suspicious vocalizers," he reported.

Though there's no way to say for sure if the animal making the suspicious vocal is a Sasquatch, it's certainly possible given the body of credible sighting reports from the area.

More recently, Ol' Mossyback may have made an appearance near Bragg Road, an infamous strip of macadam where spook lights and strange orbs have been observed for decades. The witness said that in April 2019, he and his son had been camping and were driving at a very slow rate of speed at the far north end of the road.

"As we neared the end of the road, within sight of the farm-road, a large, solid-black animal came out of the woods on the east side, walking slowly on two legs," the man explained. "It was between 7–8 feet tall and solid black."[158]

The witness said it appeared muscular with a hefty weight and bigger than a human, although it was definitely not a bear. It had long arms hanging down past its knees. He could see the details quite clearly even though he only had his parking lights on at the moment. The thing was a mere twenty feet from the car, close enough that he had to stop while the creature walked across the road.

"The scariest part of the encounter was when it paused and looked at us," the witness said. "It's eyes reflected like glowing embers when the parking lights from my truck hit it. The thing continued walking, stepping over the road grade and continuing into the forest. I stopped my truck and I could still hear it crunching around in the woods out of sight now as it walked away."

The man was frightened and started his truck again so they could leave. His fourteen-year-old son had only caught a brief glimpse of the thing as it walked into the woods because, as the witness put it, he was "playing with his #$% iPhone."

The creature was completely dark in color except for its face where it seemed to have some gray hair around the eyes and mouth, as if it were old. It was hunched over and shuffling along in no apparent hurry, seemingly indifferent to the fact that a vehicle was present.

With such an indifference to oncoming vehicles, it seems miraculous that one of these things hasn't been struck and killed. Perhaps that's just a matter of luck. In 2005, a driver crashed in the Big Thicket National Preserve while trying to avoid a man-like figure standing in the middle of the road.

On a morning in March, 2005, at 4:30 a.m., an emergency team was called to the scene of a car wreck on Highway 90 in Polk County. The road runs through the Big Thicket National Preserve where dense trees crowd both sides of the thoroughfare.[159] Upon arrival, the response team found a car rolled over and crashed into the woods. The sole passenger, the driver, was still inside. He had been knocked out by the impact, but regained consciousness at about the time the emergency personnel arrived. When asked what happened, the man said he had come upon a dark, upright figure with long hair standing in the middle of the road. He could not estimate an exact height, but it appeared to be between five and eight feet tall. The figure was unclothed with a "fuzzy face" and did not appear to be human. It was standing fully upright across the middle yellow line, facing the car.

A roadway through the Big Thicket National Preserve
(Photo by Lyle Blackburn)

The driver honked the horn, but the figure did not move. It was as if it were frozen in the headlights like a deer. When the driver got within about twenty feet, he had to swerve to avoid hitting it, which caused him to lose control and run off the road. The car hit the ditch, flipped over, and ended up in the trees.

The driver could not say for sure that this was some sort of unknown, Bigfoot-like creature, but was adamant it wasn't a human. Whatever it was, it was lucky on that particular morning. This could have been the specimen to answer all questions, though not the most desirable way in which to discover one.

As such, the mystery remains open as Ol' Mossyback and his kin continue to prowl the Texas thickets, affording an occasional glimpse or howling greeting to those brave enough or fortunate enough to trek its primordial paradise.

CONCLUSION

Several years ago I was in my local post office when a man came in and got in line behind me. There were only a few people inside at the time, so he and I were the only people waiting, aside from two women ahead of me. After a few moments, he asked if I owned the black truck with the Bigfoot sticker on the back. I confirmed that I did and introduced myself as an author who has written a few books on the subject. The man seemed both relieved that he had guessed correctly and also excited. After giving me his name, he confessed that he had most likely encountered one of the creatures a decade ago in East Texas. He said he didn't like to tell too many people about it because they tended to laugh it off, but I seemed like someone who would listen. I assured him I was.

The man proceeded to tell me about his encounter, which was consistent with many of the others we've explored in this book: wooded area, late evening, huge creature like something out of our primitive past. The witness, like many, was just as average as any Texan who might have walked into the post office that day and could easily be defined as a typical good neighbor. He seemed well educated, intelligent, and did not seem crazy or irrational. Yet he had seen something he could not explain.

When he finished telling me the details, he asked if anyone else in Texas had reported sightings. If he only knew, right? I smiled, nodded, and confirmed that indeed many people had experienced something similar here.

As we have learned in our journey across the varied regions of the state, the phenomenon of seeing a Bigfoot creature in the wilds of Texas is neither new nor rare. There have been plenty of reports, in fact—far more than I could even cover in one book. The scope of the published reports alone is far too extensive in its totality. And that's not counting the ones that have been reported to myself and my colleagues directly or those that are yet unknown. In a conservative estimate, perhaps only one in ten sightings of this type have even been reported in an official capacity. If this is true, then the phenomenon is perhaps more widespread than any of us could imagine. This goes for the whole of Bigfoot phenomena, of course, and perhaps more so for a state like Texas, where these kind of reports may seem out of place and therefore not something people are eager to report.

The reports, however, are still coming in, as what was once a mysterious campfire tale can quickly transform to stark reality in the jump of a heartbeat. Texas *is* the perfect environment for it, with settings that range from some of North America's densest thickets to remote scrublands where things can often go unnoticed in the miles of nothingness. Bigfoot may be a worldwide mystery, but it is also a decidedly Texan mystery. Cases like the ones we've examined here are just as legendary and valid as any others, far or wide.

If these creatures do exist, then naturally we must ask "What are they?" This is a question that has sparked many contrasting theories over the years, ranging from a relict hominid (ancient great ape) to a primitive form of hominin (prehuman) to an inter-dimensional being to an extraterrestrial creature from space. An exploration of these theories is beyond the scope of this book but suffice to say that anyone who is interested in this subject may have their own ideas to explain this phenomenon. It may be as simple as the creatures are lucky or as complex as the greatest physics problem on earth.

For these creatures to be ultimately proven, it will undoubtedly take more than anecdotal reports. But these are a good start to suggest there is something worth pursuing here. Legends can simply be legends, of course, but most legends don't walk around in modern times in front of average people who stroll into post offices or live next door. Sure, some of these reports could be dismissed as mistaken identity, wishful thinking, hoaxes, or tricks of light and shadow, but certainly not all of them. There are simply too many witnesses, consistent details, and history to deny that something is going on here, however strange it may be. And as my friend and colleague Craig Woolheater often says, if even one of these witnesses saw a Bigfoot, then that's enough for it to be real.

So while we're waiting for the definitive proof to come forth, such as a DNA sample or a body, we can enjoy this intriguing Texas mystery that's growing larger each day as more people embrace the subject and share their thoughts and personal accounts. Bigfoot is a big mystery and that seems to be a specialty of the Lone Star State. Somewhere among larger-than-life tales of gunslingers, oil tycoons, and heroic battles exists a creature that exemplifies the very nature of the word "big"—one that looms as large as Texas itself.

APPENDIX I: NAMES FOR BIGFOOT-LIKE CREATURES IN TEXAS

The following is a list of names used in Texas to describe Bigfoot-like creatures.

Athens Banshee
Big Cypress Swamp Monster
Boggy Bill / Hairy Bill / Skunky Bill
Brazos Ape-Man
Caddo Creature
Caddo Critter
Chambers Creek Monster
Cuthand Critter
Devil Man
El Campo Ape-Man
Hawley Him
Horizon City Monster
Hugo's Monster
Lake Worth Monster
Manimal
Marion County Monster
Night Screamer
Ol' Mossyback
Raggedy Man
Red Eyes
Sabine Thing
Sherman Gorilla
Turkey Creek Monster
Wood Ape
Wood Booger / Wooly Booger / Wooly Bugger

APPENDIX 2:
MAPS AND DATA

Geographic Regions of Texas

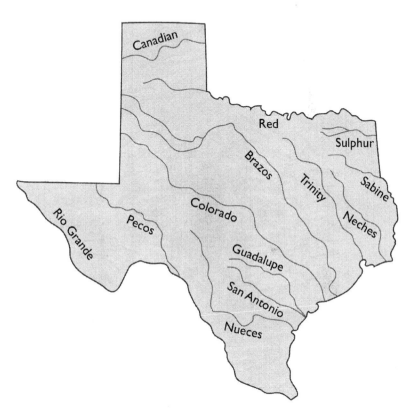

Major River Systems of Texas

Counties of Texas

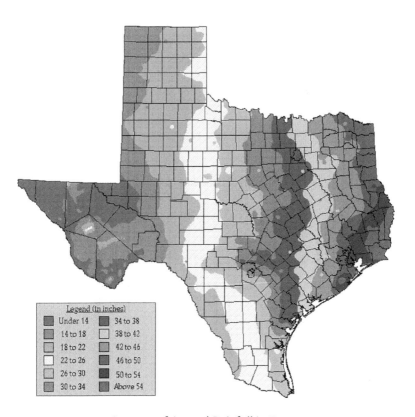

Legend (in inches)

■ Under 14	■ 34 to 38
■ 14 to 18	□ 38 to 42
□ 18 to 22	■ 42 to 46
□ 22 to 26	■ 46 to 50
□ 26 to 30	■ 50 to 54
■ 30 to 34	■ Above 54

Amount of Annual Rainfall in Texas

ACKNOWLEDGMENTS

Special recognition to the following individuals for their years of hard work and research into the subject of Bigfoot in Texas. Without them, this book would not have been possible:

Daryl Colyer, Ken Gerhard, Bobby Hamilton, Jerry Hestand, Michael Mayes, Chester Moore, and Craig Woolheater.

Thanks also to the following colleagues, friends, and family members who assisted with the research and/or otherwise contributed to the creation of this book:

Claudio Bergamin, Lyla Blackburn, Chris Buntenbah, Ashley Cheree, Charles DeVore (RIP), Glenn Haskins, Larry Parks, Monica Rawlins, Rob Riggs (RIP), Tom Shirley (RIP), Billy Simmons, Ken Stewart, and Beth Wojiski.

And most of all, I would like to thank all the eyewitnesses and organizations who graciously shared their experiences.

SOURCES

1   Cooper, Jason A. and James W. Bentley. East Texas, 2011 forest inventory and analysis factsheet. e-Science Update SRS–052. Asheville, NC: U.S. Department of Agriculture Forest Service, Southern Research Station, 2012.

2   Strain, Kathy Moskowitz. *Giants, Cannibals & Monsters: Bigfoot in Native Culture*. Washington: Hancock House Publishers, 2008.

3   "Native American Legends: Shampe." Native Languages of the Americas. (www.native-languages.org/morelegends/shampe.htm)

4   Thompson, Kyle. "The Giant Monster: Shampe." Bigfoot Encounters. (www.bigfootencounters.com/legends/shampe.htm)

5   Arment, Chad. *The Historical Bigfoot: Early Reports of Wild Men, Hairy Giants, and Wandering Gorillas in North America*. Landisville: Coachwhip Publications, 2006: p. 311.

6   Ibid., p. 313.

7   Ibid., p. 314.

8   "A Texan Orang Outang." *Michigan Argus*, (Ann Arbor, Michigan), 01 September 1871.

9   "A Wild Boy Caught." *Austin Democratic Statesman*, 21 July 1875.

10   Moses, Drew. "Park rangers spot 'Bigfoot' in Round Rock, ask kids to help track him down." *Spectrum Local News*, 19 June 2017. (https://spectrumlocalnews.com/tx/austin/news/2017/06/17/park-rangers-spot-bigfoot-in-round-rock)

11   "1836, Nacogdoches, Texas: Davy Crockett and The Bigfoot's Prophecy." Today in Bigfoot History, 15 May 2012. (https://bigfoothistory.wordpress.com/2012/05/15/1836-nacogdoches-texas-davy-crockett-and-the-bigfoots-prophecy)

12   "Texas 'Tarzan' Is Living Alone In Cave." *The News* (now The Port Arthur News), 09 February 1933.

13   "Hunt Ape Man in Brazos Area." *The Mexia Weekly* Herald, 07 April 1933.

14   Rife, Philip L. *Bigfoot Across America*. New York: Writers Club Press, 2000: p. 109.

15 Marrs, Jim. "Fishy Man-Goat Terrifies Couples Parked at Lake Worth." *Fort Worth Star-Telegram*, 10 July 1969.

16 Marrs, Jim. "Police, Residents Observe But Can't Identify 'Monster.'" *Fort Worth Star-Telegram*, 11 July 1969.

17 "'Monster' Bobcat?" *Fort Worth Star-Telegram*, 14 July 1969.

18 Kennedy, Bud. "1969 Lake Worth Monster, was the 'Goat-Man' Hulk or Hoax?" *Fort Worth Star-Telegram*, 08 June 2006.

19 Clarke, Sallie Ann. *The Lake Worth Monster*. Benbrook: self-published, 1969: p. 13.

20 Ibid., p. 14.

21 Whitley, Sean. Interview with Sallie Ann Clarke. Unpublished transcript, 2003.

22 Kennedy, Bud. "Thirty-Seven Years After Snapping Photo, Bigfoot Talk Gets Man's Goat." *Fort Worth Star-Telegram*, 08 June 2006.

23 Neal, Jim. "Hairy horror strikes again." *The Fort Worth Press*, 09 November 1969.

24 Vaughn, Chris. "Is there a Lake Worth Monster?" *Victoria Advocate*, 09 August 2009.

25 Bills, E.R. "Lake Worth Monster revealed? Goatman? *Fort Worth Magazine*, 04 July 2009.

26 "Lake Worth Goatman." Domain of Horror News Media Blogspot (now defunct).

27 Staff writer. "'Hairy Monster' Stomping Around." *Denton Record-Chronicle*, 23 July 1963.

28 "2 young people on a picnic encounter an ape-like creature." Texas Bigfoot Research Center, 26 April 2002. (Internet Archives Wayback Machine: www.texasbigfoot.com/Ellis1.html)

29 "Tall creature seen by witness." Bigfoot Field Researchers Organization, 28 June 1999. (http://www.bfro.net/GDB/show_report.asp?id=2396)

30 Redfern, Nick. "Revisiting the Chambers Creek Monster." Cryptomundo, 09 September 2013. (http://cryptomundo.com/bigfoot/revisiting-the-chambers-creek-monster)

31 Green, John. *Sasquatch: The Apes Among Us*. Washington/Vancouver: Hancock House, 1978: p. 188.

32   "Mother and son saw an upright, tall, hairy creature." Texas Bigfoot Research Center, 01 November 2004. (https://web.archive.org/web/20061111135827/http://www.texasbigfoot.com/Henderson4.html)

33   "Tall, white, hairy creature seen." Texas Bigfoot Research Center, 27 August 2002. (https://web.archive.org/web/20061111135827/http://.texasbigfoot.com/Henderson2.html)

34   Ibid.

35   "Early 1970's – Large ape man attacks man's home, tears piece of roof off." Gulf Coast Bigfoot Research Organization. (http://gcbro.com/Txrob001.htm)

36   "Early 1970's – Man plowing fields is chased off tractor by ape man." Gulf Coast Bigfoot Research Organization. (http://gcbro.com/Txrob002.htm)

37   "Early 1970's – Man riding horse chased by ape like creature." Gulf Coast Bigfoot Research Organization. (http://gcbro.com/Txrob003.htm)

38   "November 21, 2007 – Woman driving home from work late at night sees a Bigfoot creature." Gulf Coast Bigfoot Research Organization. (http://www.gcbro.com/TXrobertson0004.html)

39   Sicking, Jennifer. "'Haunted bridge' moves to Callisburg Wednesday." *Gainesville Daily Register*, 3 June 2004.

40   "Youth has sighting near bridge." Texas Bigfoot Research Center, 27 December 2004. (https://web.archive.org/web/20061111135827/http://www.texasbigfoot.com/Cooke3.html)

41   Hestand, Jerry. *Hunting Apes in America: My Life as a Bigfoot Hunter.* Arizona/Missouri: Moon Pigeon Publishing, 2017: pp. 224, 225.

42   Jacobs, Willie. "Huge Ape Reported Seen At Blue Creek." *Sherman Democrat*, 20 July 1960.

43   Jacobs, Willie. "Policeman Recalls Night Elephant Got Loose Here." *Sherman Democrat*, 31 July 1960.

44   Perez, Daniel and Jerry Hestand. "Follow Up." *Bigfoot Times* March 2017: p. 2.

45   Ibid.

46   "Direct Has Critter Too." *The Paris News*, (day/month unknown) 1965.

47 "Sightings near Pat Mayse Lake." Texas Bigfoot Research Center, 19 March 2002. (https://web.archive.org/web/20061111135827/http://www.texasbigfoot.com/Lamar4.html)

48 "Bigfoot seen in creek near Powderly." Texas Bigfoot Research Center, 18 March 2002. (https://web.archive.org/web/20061111135827/http://www.texasbigfoot.com/Lamar3.html)

49 "2 women see a Bigfoot cross road in front of them." Texas Bigfoot Research Center, 29 April 2002. (https://web.archive.org/web/20061111135827/http://www.texasbigfoot.com/Lamar6.html)

50 "Sighting in Lamar County." Texas Bigfoot Research Center. January 31, 2007. Unpublished.

51 Holley, David. "The Cuthand Critter." Scary Sasquatch Stories. (www.network54.com/Forum)

52 While searching for their uncle, two boys have visual encounter." North American Wood Ape Conservancy. (http://woodape.org/reports/report/detail/127)

53 Ibid.

54 "Bigfoot observed crossing road." Gulf Coast Bigfoot Research Organization. (http://gcbro.com/TXredriv001.htm)

55 Jones, Mark and Teresa Ann Smith. "Has Bigfoot Moved To Texas?" *FATE* July 1979: 30–36.

56 Ibid.

57 "Driver reports late night road encounter at Sulphur River near Commerce." North American Wood Ape Conservancy. (https://reports.woodape.org/data/?action=details&case=01020049#CaseNum)

58 "Woman taking a walk has startling encounter near the Sulphur River." North American Wood Ape Conservancy. (http://woodape.org/reports/report/detail/294)

59 "Father and son report nighttime road cross encounter in Sulphur River bottoms. Texas Bigfoot Research Center, 05 October, 2005. (https://web.archive.org/web/20061111135827/http://www.texasbigfoot.com/Hunt5.html)

60 "Delta Co. sighting report." Texas Bigfoot Research Center archives, 07 August 2003. Unpublished.

61   "1980's–1995,between Commerce and Cooper, TX ; Bigfoot sightings and track finds." Texas Bigfoot Research Center. (https://web.archive.org/web/20061111135827/http://www.texasbigfoot.com/Delta2.html)

62   Roller, Cindy. "Bigfoot or Kangaroo? You decide." *Cooper Review,* 29 October 2015.

63   "Report from Knights Bluff." The files of Charles DeVore.

64   "Deer hunter reports encounter in Sulphur River bottoms at western edge of Wright-Patman Lake." North American Wood Ape Conservancy. (https://reports.woodape.org/data/?action=details&case=01030013#CaseNum)

65   "Mother, children and friend of family have road encounter near Atlanta on Highway 59." North American Wood Ape Conservancy. (https://reports.woodape.org/data/?action=details&case=01080120#CaseNum)

66   Ibid.

67   "Encounter during a summer camp campout near the Brazos River." Bigfoot Field Researchers Organization, 13 April 2006. (www.bfro.net/GDB/show_report.asp?id=14376)

68   "Several Bigfoot incidents during this span." Texas Bigfoot Research Center (https://web.archive.org/web/20061111135827/http://www.texasbigfoot.com/PaloPinto.html), 05 March 2002.

69   Lynch, Lee. "Strange Footprints in Palo Pinto County." Personal notes supplied to the author. 28 February 2013.

70   Bord, Janet and Colin Bord. *Bigfoot Casebook Updated: Sightings and Encounters from 1818 to 2004.* Pine Winds Press, an imprint of Idyll Arbor, 2006 (first published in 1982): p. 279.

71   "'Big Foot' Terrorizes Kelly Area." *The San Antonio Light,* 01 September 1976.

72   Gerhard, Ken and Nick Redfern. *Monsters of Texas.* North Devon, England: CFZ Press, 2010: pp. 54–55.

73   "Tall hairy figure leans out from behind a tree to observe woman outside San Antonio." Bigfoot Field Researchers Organization, 18 August 2008. (http://www.bfro.net/GDB/show_report.asp?id=24529)

74   City of San Antonio Police Department. Audio, 911 call. November 30, 2009.

75   City of San Antonio Police Department. November 30, 2009. *Complainant/Reported by Jennifer.*

76   Mayes, Michael. "The San Antonio Sasquatch Investigation." Texas Cryptid Hunter. 10 December 2009 (http://texascryptidhunter.blogspot.com/2009/12/san-antonio-sasquatch-investigation.html)

77   Ibid.

78   "Texas Hill Country, Bandera County, Texas." Bigfoot Encounters. (www.bigfootencounters.com)

79   "Early evening sighting near a home and strange deer kills investigated at Canyon Lake." Bigfoot Field Researchers Organization, 18 January 2015. (www.bfro.net/GDB/show_report.asp?id=47702)

80   Dennett, Michael. "Experiments Cast Doubt on Bigfoot 'Evidence.'" *Skeptical Inquirer*, 01 September 2006.

81   Bruce, Bob. "Caddo's 'Critter Jitters' Aren't Total: But Those Who Have 'Em Are Convinced." *The Abilene Reporter-News*, 22 July 1964.

82   Ibid.

83   Kellam, George. "Haskell Rascal Plain Varmint, Say Experts." *Fort Worth Star-Telegram*, 14 June 1963.

84   "Camera Catches 'Critter.'" *Fort Worth Star-Telegram*, 01 August 1964.

85   "It's Man, Monster, Nothing." *Fort Worth Star-Telegram*, 03 August 1964.

86   "Yak About Caddo Critter Quieted by Area Ranch." *Abilene Reporter-News*, 23 July 1964.

87   "Bigfoot Attack in Texas 1994." Dixie Cryptid. (https://www.youtube.com/watch?v=kQh6blFFKlw)

88   Downing, Roger. "Youths Report Attack By the 'Hawley Him.'" *Abilene Reporter-News*, 07 July 1977.

89   Duff, Katharyn. "Hunters Seek Sniff of 'Hawley Him.' *Abilene Reporter-News*, 08 July 1977.

90   Downing, Roger. "Abilenians Go to Hawley to Hunt 'Him.'" *Abilene Reporter-News*, 07 July 1977.

91   "Reward Offered For Creature." *The Altus Times Democrat*, 17 August 1977.

92 "Large Creature Seen on Bridge." Gulf Coast Bigfoot Researchers Organization. (www.gcbro.com/TXjones001.html)

93 "Three bikers returning from Mexico have strange road encounter near Muleshoe Wildlife Refuge." North American Wood Ape Conservancy. (https://reports.woodape.org/data/?action=details&case=01050029#CaseNum)

94 Bugs. "I Shot Bigfoot." Interviewed by Art Bell. *Coast To Coast AM*, aired 05 June 2001. (www.coasttocoastam.com/show/i-shot-bigfoot)

95 Coleman, Loren. "Bugs Bigfoot Legend Begun By Radio Freakazoid." Cryptozoo News, 07 January 2009. (www.cryptozoonews.com/bugs-freakazoid)

96 Moore, Bill. "His Face Is Pushed In And His Ears 'Point.'" *El Paso Times*, 20 September 1975.

97 "El Paso Incident Report." Texas Bigfoot Research Center. December 29, 2003. Unpublished.

98 Chávez, Adriana M. "Some residents believe in Horizon City's monster." *El Paso Times*, 31 July 2003.

99 Power, Irvin. "Boy Says For Real Sighting of Monster Renews Marion Legend." *Marshall News Messenger*, 01 September 1965.

100 "Hairy Monster Leaves New Track." *Pittsburg Gazette* (Texas), (day/month unknown) 1968.

101 Ibid.

102 "Marion County 'Monster' Recalls 1927 Experience." *Longview News-Journal*, 09 September 1965.

103 "Town Fed Up With Monster Hunters." *United Press International*, 20 September 1965.

104 "Concerning the Longview, Texas, Reports." *Bigfoot Bulletin* 31 October 1970: p. 3.

105 Strain, Kathy Moskowitz. *Giants, Cannibals & Monsters: Bigfoot in Native Culture*. Washington: Hancock House Publishers, 2008.

106 "Teenage girl recalls late night road encounter near Caddo Lake." Texas Bigfoot Research Center, 25 February 2006. (https://web.archive.org/web/20061111135827/http://www.texasbigfoot.com/Harrison10.html)

107 "Deer hunter encounters bigfoot at Caddo Lake near Karnack." Bigfoot Field Researchers Organization, 22 February 2004. (www.bfro.net/GDB/show_report.asp?id=8067)

108 "Ongoing encounters with a Bigfoot on family property at Caddo Lake." Texas Bigfoot Research Center, 25 February 2004. (https://web.archive.org/web/20061111135827/http://www.texasbigfoot.com/Harrison8.html)

109 Ibid.

110 "Dr. Carl Baugh examines suspected Bigfoot evidence." Texas Bigfoot Research Center archives, 2003. Unpublished.

111 "Woman reports visual encounter near Little Cypress Bayou on Highway 154." North American Wood Ape Conservancy. (https://reports.woodape.org/data/?action=details&case=01020056#CaseNum)

112 Roadside visual encounter on FM 1997 west of Woodlawn." North American Wood Ape Conservancy. (https://reports.woodape.org/data/?action=details&case=01010007#CaseNum)

113 "Family reports visual encounter while target shooting near an open pasture." North American Wood Ape Conservancy. (http://woodape.org/reports/report/detail/136)

114 Bord, Janet and Colin Bord. *Bigfoot Casebook Updated: Sightings and Encounters from 1818 to 2004.* Pine Winds Press, an imprint of Idyll Arbor, 2006 (first published in 1982): p. 202.

115 Able, Charles. "Do creatures lurk in East Texas creek bottoms?" *Longview News-Journal,* 28 November 1976.

116 "Bowfishermen have early afternoon encounter while on Sabine River." North American Wood Ape Conservancy (http://woodape.org/reports/report/detail/446)

117 "Nurse has early-morning highway encounter near Lake Murvaul." North American Wood Ape Conservancy (https://reports.woodape.org/data/?action=details&case=01090093#CaseNum)

118 "Encounter on Toledo Bend." Bigfoot Field Researchers Organization, 12 January 2001. (www.bfro.net/GDB/show_report.asp?id=1213)

119 "Sabine County sighting report." Texas Bigfoot Research Center archives, September 22, 2003. Unpublished.

120 Ibid.

121 "Hunters see 8'–8.5' brownish black Bigfoot, standing in a clump of trees watching them." Gulf Coast Bigfoot Research Organization. (http://gcbro.com/Txnew001.htm)

122 Whitney, Andrea. "Hauntings and Legends: Does Bigfoot live in Newton Co.?" *The Jasper Newsboy*, 04 October 2017.

123 Meaux, Mary. "Bigfoot sighting along Neches River?" *The Port Arthur News*, 19 February 2013.

124 Mayes, Michael. "Possible Sasquatch Tracks Located in SE Texas." Texas Cryptid Hunter, 10 May 2010. (http://texascryptidhunter.blogspot.com/2010/05/possible-sasquatch-tracks-located-in-se.html)

125 "Woman tells of her husband's close encounter as a young man with 'The Hermit' near Huntsville." Bigfoot Field Researchers Organization, 6 April 2008. (www.bfro.net/gdb/show_report.asp?id=23531)

126 "Girl reports having visual encounter while rowing a boat across a lake in Huntsville State Park." North American Wood Ape Conservancy. (https://reports.woodape.org/data/?action=details&case=01000002#CaseNum)

127 Hestand, Jerry. *Hunting Apes in America: My Life as a Bigfoot Hunter.* Arizona/Missouri: Moon Pigeon Publishing, 2017: pp. 178-180.

128 Ibid., p. 176.

129 "Predawn encounter on east side of FM 1375 bridge over Lake Conroe." North American Wood Ape Conservancy. (http://woodape.org/reports/report/detail/225)

130 "Husband and wife observe massive upright animal in Sam Houston National Forest." North American Wood Ape Conservancy. (http://woodape.org/reports/report/detail/26894)

131 "Hunters see four-foot tall bipedal black hair covered creature leave area in a hasty retreat." Gulf Coast Bigfoot Research Organization. (http://gcbro.com/Txsanj002.htm)

132 Green, John. Sasquatch Database. Defunct.

133 "Motorist recounts daylight sighting on her property east of New Waverly." Bigfoot Field Researchers Organization, 17 February 2011. (www.bfro.net/GDB/show_report.asp?id=28873)

134 "Photographer's daylight encounter west of Coldspring in Sam Houston National Forest." Bigfoot Field Researchers Organization, 22 September 2019. (www.bfro.net/GDB/show_report.asp?id=63398)

135 "Worker has early morning visual encounter while working on construction of Fox Sports Facility." North American Wood Ape Conservancy. (http://woodape.org/reports/report/detail/1493)

136 "On duty security officer has early morning encounter at construction facility." North American Wood Ape Conservancy. (http://woodape.org/reports/report/detail/439)

137 "Woman reports sighting from highway while riding as passenger." North American Wood Ape Conservancy. (http://woodape.org/reports/report/detail/432)

138 Chesna's Footage Room. "Texas Bigfoot – Danny Sweeten." YouTube. *Strange Universe*. December 20, 2018. (https://youtu.be/scfQZJG-PHRs)

139 Ibid.

140 Ibid.

141 McNabb, Scott. "The Danny Sweeten Case." Bigfoot Encounters (http://www.bigfootencounters.com/hoaxes/sweeten.htm)

142 Ibid.

143 "Students see a Bigfoot near their campsite." Texas Bigfoot Research Center, 2 August 2002. (https://web.archive.org/web/20061111135827/http://www.texasbigfoot.com/Angelina5.html)

144 "Couple in car encounter a strange creature." Texas Bigfoot Research Center, 23 August 2003. (https://web.archive.org/web/20061111135827/http://www.texasbigfoot.com/Angelina8.html)

145 "2 hunters saw a large, 2 legged ape looking creature." Texas Bigfoot Research Center, 15 December 2001. (https://web.archive.org/web/20061111135827/http://www.texasbigfoot.com/Angelina1.html)

146 Riggs, Rob. *In the Big Thicket: On the Trail of the Wild Man*. New York: Paraview Press, 2001.

147 "Squirrel hunter has a daytime encounter." Texas Bigfoot Research Center, 16 January 2005. (https://web.archive.org/web/20061111135827/http://www.texasbigfoot.com/Liberty.html)

148 "i-dineout.com: Dayton Monkey Man." Texas Bigfoot Research Center, 15 July 2003. (https://web.archive.org/web/20061111135827/http://www.texasbigfoot.com/idineout.html)

149 Ibid.

150 "Bigfoot observed possibly feeding on carcass in middle of Highway 105 near the Trinity River." Texas Bigfoot Research Center, 3 April 2004. (https://web.archive.org/web/20061111135827/http://www.texasbigfoot.com/Liberty1.html)

151 "El Campo Ape Man." Unknown Explorers. (www.unknownexplorers.com/elcampoapeman.php)

152 Cockburn, Harry. "Mystery humanoid cat-snatching creature 'spotted' running wild and attacking children in Texas." The Independent, 11 September 2019. (https://www.independent.co.uk/news/world/americas/monkey-texas-santa-fe-chimpanzee-cat-attack-police-a9100836.html)

153 "Eyes on Texas: Big Thicket National Preserve." Durango Texas website. (www.durangotexas.com/eyesontexas/TexasRegions/PineyWoods/big%20thicket.htm)

154 Riggs, Rob. *In the Big Thicket: On the Trail of the Wild Man.* New York: Paraview Press, 2001.

155 "Witness spots a large, dark, hairy creature standing 50 yards away." Bigfoot Field Researchers Organization, 9 November 1997. (http://www.bfro.net/GDB/show_report.asp?id=4141)

156 "November 1999: Lady fears for her child's safety while out picnicking due to his newfound hairy friend." Gulf Coast Bigfoot Research Organization. (www.gcbro.com/TXpolk004.htm)

157 "2001, Woodville, TX; Woman sees a Bigfoot in her backyard. Texas Bigfoot Research Center, 21 July 2002. (https://web.archive.org/web/20061111135827/http://www.texasbigfoot.com/Tyler1.html)

158 "Sighting by motorist 10 miles SE of Big Thicket National Preserve." Bigfoot Field Researchers Organization, 16 April 2019. (www.bfro.net/GDB/show_report.asp?id=62746)

159 "Single car accident in Big Thicket National Preserve." Bigfoot Field Researchers Organization, 08 May 2005. (www.bfro.net/GDB/show_report.asp?id=11635)

INDEX

A

Abilene Boys' Ranch, 116

Alamo, 3, 5, 18, 19, 98, 194

Amarillo, 122, 125, 128

American Monster Tour, 156

Anderson Creek, 74

Angelina County, 213

Angelina National Forest,
208, 209, 210, 214

Argo, 78

Ash Creek, 40

Athens, 43, 45, 233

Athens Banshee, 43, 233

Atlanta (Texas), 79, 80, 245

Austin, 15, 16, 208, 241

B

Bagwell, 69, 70

Baily County, 124

Bandera County, 104, 246

Bayou Bodcau, 154

Beckville, 168, 169

Bedias Creek, 195

Big Cypress Bayou, 148, 149, 150

Big Sandy Creek, 222

Big Thicket, 191, 194, 215,
219, 220, 222, 224, 225,
226, 228, 250, 251

Black Cypress Creek, 144

Blackland Prairies, 86, 98

Block Bayou, 183

Blue Creek, 61, 63, 66, 243

Bluff Creek, 156

Boggy Creek, 73

Boggy Creek Monster.
See Fouke Monster

Boggy Creek: The Legend
Is True, 154

Bowie County, 74

Bragg Road, 225

Brazos River, 22, 49, 50, 86,
88, 89, 90, 93, 245

Brushy Creek, 17

C

Caddo Creature, 147,
148, 155, 193, 233

Caddo Critter, 112, 113, 114,
115, 116, 148, 233, 246

Caddo Lake, 138, 147, 148,
149, 150, 152, 153, 154, 155,
156, 157, 158, 247, 248

Caddo (town), 113, 114, 115

Caddo tribe, 11, 56, 148

Callisburg, 57, 58, 59, 60, 243

Calvert, 49, 50

Canyon Lake, 105, 246

Carlsbad Caverns, 134

Carthage, 4, 167, 169

Cass County, 157

Cedar Hill, 22

cemetery, 140, 141, 185, 220

Chambers Creek, 43, 44, 233, 242

Chambers Creek Monster, 43, 233, 242

Choctaw Creek, 64

Choctaw (tribe), 11, 64

Chupacabra, 129

Clarke, Sallie Ann, 31, 33, 242

Cleburne, 22

Cleveland (Texas), 204

Coast To Coast AM, 126, 206, 247

Commerce, 72, 74, 244, 245

Cooke County, 57, 58

Cooper Lake, 75, 76

Corsicana, 44

Creation Evidence Museum, 157

Creature from Black Lake, 154, 155

Crockett, Davy, 5, 18, 19, 21, 51, 194, 241

Cuthand Creek, 68, 69

Cuthand Critter, 68, 233, 244

D

Dallas, 22, 41, 42, 43, 107, 108

Davy Crockett National Forest, 51

Dayton, 214, 215, 216, 218, 251

Decatur, 36

Delta County, 75, 76, 244

Denton, 36, 242

Devil's Elbow, 149, 153

Direct, 66, 67, 68, 69, 243

E

El Campo Ape-Man, 233

Ellis County, 22, 38, 43, 130, 131

El Paso, 4, 112, 129, 130, 132, 134, 135, 166, 247

F

FATE magazine, 72, 244

federal agents, 128

Finding Bigfoot (television show), 42, 155

Fort Worth, 3, 4, 22, 27, 28, 30, 31, 32, 34, 37, 39, 41, 42, 86, 114, 242, 246

Fouke Monster, 10, 56, 57, 71, 83, 187

G

Gatesville, 15, 16

ghost, 3, 35, 46, 58, 90

Glen Rose, 157

goatman, 29, 35, 36, 242

gorilla, 33, 34, 62, 63, 64, 65, 66, 68, 73, 80, 89, 93, 94, 112, 113, 114, 132, 141, 200, 203, 205, 213

Grand Prairie, 41, 42, 43, 197

Grapeland, 51

Grapevine, 39, 42

graveyard. *See* cemetery

Grayson County, 58, 62, 63, 64

Gulf Coast, 4, 49, 210, 212, 218, 221, 243, 244, 247, 249, 251

Gulf of Mexico, 26, 183, 195

H

Hagerman Wildlife Refuge, 59

Hallsville, 162

Harrison County, 150, 161

Haskell, 114, 116, 246

Hawley, 116, 118, 119, 121, 233, 246

Hawley Him, 116, 118, 119, 121, 233, 246

Henderson County, 44

Hills Lake, 167

Horizon City, 129, 131, 132, 133, 134, 135, 233, 247

Horizon City Monster, 129, 131, 132, 135, 233

Houston, 13, 14, 22, 192, 194, 195, 197, 199, 202, 204, 249, 250

Howco International Pictures, 154

Hugo's Monster, 89, 93, 94, 233

Hunt County, 75, 106, 110, 155, 241, 246

Huntsville, 195, 196, 249

Huntsville State Park, 196, 249

J

jaguarundi, 159

Jeems Bayou, 148, 152

Jefferson, 138, 139, 140, 142, 143, 146, 147, 148, 153, 154, 159, 161, 162

K

Kelly Air Force Base, 99

Killing Bigfoot (television show), 212

Knight's Bluff, 78

Kyle Mountain, 93, 94

L

Lake Conroe, 197, 198, 249

Lake of the Pines, 159, 160

Lake Raven, 196

Lake Worth, 27, 36, 40, 242

Lake Worth Monster, 26, 27, 29, 30, 31, 33, 35, 36, 37, 47, 233, 242

Lamar County, 66, 68, 244

Lavaca County, 12, 14

Legend of Boggy Creek, The, 57, 71, 84, 154, 187, 188

Liberty County, 216, 217, 250

Little Cypress Bayou, 148, 248

Longview, 141, 142, 143, 162, 247, 248

M

Manimal, 66, 67, 68, 69, 233

Marion County, 138, 139, 140, 141, 142, 143, 144, 147, 157, 193, 233, 247

Marion County Monster, 139, 141, 142, 157, 193, 233

Marshall, 140, 162, 163, 247

Matagorda County, 218

Maud, 79

Mineral Wells, 90

monkey, 30, 35, 52, 188, 199, 215, 216, 217, 218, 221, 251

Monsters & Mysteries in America (television show), 30

Montgomery County, 195, 201

Muleshoe National Wildlife Refuge, 124

Murvaul Creek, 171

N

Nacogdoches County, 210, 241

Native American, 8, 10, 241

Navarro County, 43

Navidad River, 12, 14

Newton County, 179, 180, 187, 249

O

Oil City, 154

Ol' Mossyback, 219, 225, 227, 233

orangutan, 15, 223

P

Pacific Northwest, 2, 3, 5, 9, 87, 119, 157, 208

Palo Pinto County, 88, 92, 93, 94, 97, 245

Panola County, 167, 168, 169, 171, 172, 173

Paris (Texas), 66, 243

Pat Mayse Lake, 66, 244

Peavy Switch, 209, 210

Phantom Hill, 119, 120

Pine Creek, 67

Pine Island Bayou, 219

Polk County, 220, 222, 225, 226

Port Arthur, 22, 183, 241, 249

Port Neches, 183

Possum Kingdom, 86, 88, 90, 91, 94

Q

Queen City, 78

R

Red Oak, 23, 36

Red River County, 68, 69

Richland-Chambers Reservoir, 44

Richmond, 22

Robertson County, 49, 50

Round Rock, 16, 17, 18, 241

S

Sabine National Forest, 178

Sabine River, 162, 166, 167, 171, 173, 177, 178, 183, 187, 211, 248

Sabine Thing, 166, 173, 179, 233

Sam Houston National Forest, 192, 194, 195, 199, 204, 249, 250

San Antonio, 98, 99, 100, 101, 102, 103, 104, 106, 245, 246

San Antonio River, 98

Sandy Creek, 57, 222

San Jacinto County, 195, 199

San Marcos, 15, 16

Santa Fe (Texas), 218

Shampe, 11, 241

Shamrock, 128

Sherman, 60, 61, 62,
64, 65, 233, 243

Sherman Gorilla, 60, 233

Skookum: The Hunt for Bigfoot, 155

Startzville, 105

states:

Alabama, 11

Arkansas, 10, 11, 56, 57, 71, 73,
82, 84, 127, 138, 148

Florida, 11

Mississippi, 11

New Mexico, 112, 129, 134

Oklahoma, 8, 11, 56, 58, 70, 122,
138

Stephen F. Austin State
University, 208

Strange Universe, 203, 205, 250

T

Texarkana, 57, 78

Texas Bigfoot Conference, 1, 138

Texas Department of
Public Safety, 76

Texas Highways magazine, 125, 201

Texas National Guard, 143

Texas Parks and Wildlife
Department, 208

Thickett Branch, 195

Toledo Bend Reservoir, 178

Town Creek, 95

Trinity River, 26, 28, 39, 41, 42, 43,
47, 49, 51, 53, 215, 217, 219, 251

Tyler County, 221

V

video, 203, 204, 205, 206, 207

W

Waco, 49

Walker County, 142, 195

Woodlands, The, 202

Woodlawn, 160, 161, 248

Worth Ranch, 90, 91

Wright Patman Lake, 78, 82

ABOUT THE AUTHOR

Lyle Blackburn is a native Texan known for his work in writing, music, and film. He is the author of several acclaimed books, including The Beast of Boggy Creek and Sinister Swamps, whose subject matter reflects his life-long fascination with cryptid creatures and strange phenomena. Lyle is also the founder of the rock band, Ghoultown, and narrator/co-producer of documentary films including *The Mothman of Point Pleasant* and *Boggy Creek Monster*. Lyle is a frequent guest speaker at cryptozoology and paranormal conferences around the country and has appeared on numerous television shows such as *Monsters and Mysteries in America*, *Strange Evidence*, *The UnXplained*, and *Finding Bigfoot*.

For more information, visit www.lyleblackburn.com

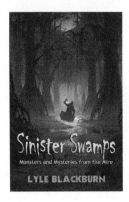
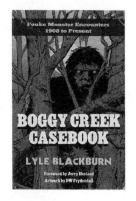

MORE BOOKS BY THE AUTHOR

The Beast of Boggy Creek:
The True Story of the Fouke Monster

Beyond Boggy Creek:
In Search of the Southern Sasquatch

Lizard Man:
The True Story of the Bishopville Monster

Momo:
The Strange Case of the Missouri Monster

Sinister Swamps:
Monsters and Mysteries from the Mire

Boggy Creek Casebook:
Fouke Monster Encounters 1908 to Present

Monstro Bizarro:
An Essential Manual of Mysterious Monsters

legend
SCAPE

Made in the USA
Monee, IL
16 January 2023

25410523R00157